# FINANCE CAPITAL

# IMPERIALISM

### And

# WAR

Alexander Koh, 1927

Svitlana M, Erdogan A

The book is the translation of Financial Capital by Alexander Koh written and printed in Soviets at 1927

Statistical data from the book are not translated, to keep the book short. The context and explanations are found to be sufficient to have the fundamental understanding of the emergence of financial capital, its policy of imperialism and inevitability of war.

As always; There is no copyright.

Purpose is to share, make available and accessible what we study rather than keeping to ourselves.

# CONTENT

## FROM THE AUTHOR

## MOBILIZATION OF CAPITAL.

1. Distribution of the joint-stock form of enterprises

2. Reasons for the spread of joint-stock companies

3. Joint-stock form of the enterprise

4. Constituent profits

5. Issue of bonds

6. Joint stock company as an instrument of domination of large capitals over small ones

7. The system of "subsidiaries, enterprises.

## NEW ROLE OF BANKS.

8. Banks as organizational centers of industrial slapping.

9. Banking concerns

10. Concentration of banks

11. Merging industrial capital with credit ..

12. Society for funding ... ... .

13. Industrial concerns. Stinnes Concern

## CAPITALIST MONOPOLIES.

14. Syndicates, cartels, trusts, capitalist monopoly

15. Financial-capitalist state

## IMPERIALISM.

## FROM THE AUTHOR TO THE FIRST EDITION

The study of modern, i.e., financial capitalism, must constitute, and to some extent already constitutes, the main part of the course of political economy in our general education schools, as well as in party schools and Komsomol universities. Meanwhile, in our book market there are still no textbooks for this most important part of the course.

The present work is an attempt, at least in part, to fill this gap.

Our book is a teaching aid and only a teaching aid. The author, of course, does not claim originality or independence of the conclusions - the work is based on the Leninist concept.

## TO THE SECOND EDITION.

Being loaded with current work, I am unfortunately unable to make all those corrections in this edition.

And the additions required by the work before the reader. I am compelled to confine myself to the most necessary corrections, without which certain parts of the book would lose interest.

This edition contains a number of corrections and a number of insertions in 4, 5, 9, 14, 15, 19, 22 and especially in 12, 1 3, 17 and 21; the general layout of the material has been changed, a number of diagrams have been added, and the diagram of the division of the world, attached at the end of the book, has been reworked.

## MOBILIZATION OF CAPITAL

Spread of the joint-stock form of enterprises, a characteristic feature of modern capitalism is the extensive development and spread of the network of joint-stock companies. Joint stock companies as a form of organization of enterprises, are not the product of the last decades of capitalist development. Historians of the economy attribute their appearance to the 17th (and some even to the 15th) century. However, during this period, joint-stock companies appear very rarely, and besides, they differ very little from ordinary partnerships on shares. Since the second half of the 19th century, and especially since the beginning of the 20th century, joint-stock companies in their developed form have become the predominant form of enterprises in a number of industries, turning into an encouraging way to invest large capital.

The development of a network of joint-stock companies in Russia is drawn as follows:

*(statistical data)*

We see that joint-stock companies, which almost did not spread until the eighties of the last century, show since then a tendency to intensive distribution; their number increases more than five times in 31 years, and their capital seven times in 23 years.

In Germany, the number of joint-stock companies and their power grew as follows:

*(statistical data)*

We see not only how rapidly the number of joint-stock companies is growing, but also how joint-stock companies are turning into the predominant form of enterprise, how their share in social production is increasing.

By 1919, joint-stock companies concentrated on their premises 86.5% of all workers employed in the industry of the United States. They produced in their factories and factories 87.1% of all industrial output in this country. These figures are enough to agree that joint-stock companies have become the dominant form of production here.

We cannot provide equally well-developed data on the share of joint-stock companies in the production of other countries. However, indirectly, we are convinced that there, too, joint-stock companies have achieved an undoubted predominance in production.

(Statistics)

We see that the overwhelming majority of equity capital is rushing into the largest, i.e., the most advanced enterprises that play an exceptional role in the modern economy. As can be seen from Table 7, these largest enterprises in Germany are overwhelmingly in the hands of joint-stock companies.

The growth rate of the capital of joint-stock companies turns out to be much faster than in non-stock industry. If at the beginning of the period covered by the table most of the capital was invested in non-stock companies, then at the end of its period the capital of joint-stock companies is more than twice the total capital of the privately owned factory and cottage industry.

**Reasons for the spread of joint-stock companies.**

The second half of the 19th century and the beginning of the 20th century were marked by an unprecedented growth in technology. "Never before has man's dominance over external nature reached even approximately such a degree of development as in a given period of time, and such a radical revolution in the foundations of production technology has not been accomplished so quickly."

"The victory over time and space is a revolution of transport and communications, bringing together the continents and opening up the most remote corners of the earth for modern industry; victorious penetration into all areas of life by the new energy of the future-electricity, which now makes it possible to throw grandiose energy flows over hundreds of miles, turn them into any of the forms and crush them to practically infinitesimal values;

oil engines, which also make it easy to transport, crush and rationally use the life-giving sources of life, a legacy of past geological eras; the simultaneous improvement of steam technology, which still does not give up without a struggle, the rapid quantitative and qualitative development of mechanical engineering, which turns individual mechanisms into almost animated beings, and, most importantly, throws masses of these "steel slaves" on the earth, replacing millions of people now;

finally, the successes of industrial chemistry, which synthetically creates the most complex organic compounds on a large scale and has come close to the problem of the artificial synthesis of proteins - such is a small part of the successes of modern technology" . (M. Rubinstein).

This gigantic development of technology over the past 50-75 years could not but exert a powerful influence on the economic life of peoples. The development of technology accelerates the process of concentration of production. New inventions can be introduced, the production process can be mechanized from beginning to end only by those enterprises that have sufficiently large capital at their disposal. As technology develops, the big enterprises thus find themselves in the hands of an increasingly powerful weapon, with which they destroy and oust their weaker competitors from production. Looking closely at the industrial statistics of the principal capitalist countries, we easily notice two closely related processes:

1) the process of the relative displacement of small enterprises by large ones,

2) the process of consolidation of medium-sized enterprises.

(Stat)

We see that the number of small enterprises is relatively declining. The number of medium and large enterprises is increasing. At the same time, it is important to note that the number of large enterprises is growing faster, while the number of medium-sized ones is growing more slowly.

Except for the unexpected rise in 1909, all the other years taken show a very distinct downward trend in the average rate of turnover of capital. Over the 45 years under consideration, the rate of turnover of social capital has decreased by almost 2 times.

Here we are witnessing the process of "binding" capital, linking it in P. JO Production.

Whereas in 1869 the average American capitalist needed $6,700 to set up an enterprise, in 1914 he needed $82,600 for the same purpose, i.e., 13 times more.

At the same time, in 1869 he invested his capital, on average, for ½ of the year, in 1914 for the whole year.

The growth of the average size of the capital of the enterprise and the "binding

» it in production and are the main reason for the spread of the joint-stock form of the enterprise.

Joint-stock companies are a form of organization of enterprises that provides employees with

capital the maximum degree of mobility (mobility).

They give the capitalist, who has invested his capital in an industrial, commercial, or banking enterprise, the opportunity at any moment to withdraw this capital from the enterprise and, moreover, in the form of money. The capitalist who participates today in a mining enterprise may tomorrow become a participant in a railroad company, and the day after tomorrow throw his capital into trade. in a machine-building plant, a weaving factory, an electric station.

Such mobility (mobility) of capital. is a property of joint-stock companies only. An individual entrepreneur, having invested his capital in any enterprise, cannot withdraw it until the end of the full turnover. The more constrained the mobility of capital in production, the more the desire on the part of the capitalists to investing capital not in individual, but in joint-stock enterprises. That is why the joint-stock form of enterprises extends primarily to the largest enterprises. This is confirmed by the fact that the development of joint-stock companies is especially intensified precisely in those spheres of economic life where the capital necessary for running an enterprise is especially large or where fixed capital constitutes a significant part of the total capital.

(statistical data)

We see that the enterprises of these four groups have just the largest capitals. The data presented serve as undoubted proof of the idea that it is precisely the growth of the average size of capital and its binding in production that is the reason for the spread of the joint-stock form of enterprises.

## Shareholding form of the enterprise.

The process of expansion of joint-stock companies significantly changes capitalist relations, regenerates the cellular tissue of the capitalist organism. Its immediate result is the bringing of social capital into a mobile state - the abundance of capital.

The capital of a joint-stock company, both in form and in its essence, is social capital. The capital necessary for the organization of the enterprise is collected by subscription throughout the country or even around the world.

A group of founder capitalists (in most cases a bank) announces the organization of a joint-stock company. A certain number of shares are issued, which can be purchased (buy) by anyone. The proceeds from the sale of shares form the capital of the joint-stock company. Each shareholder (shareholder) is considered one of the co-owners of the enterprise and has the right to receive a part of the company's annual profit (dividend).

However, the property rights of each shareholder within a joint-stock company are limited, firstly, by the fact that he does not have the right to demand the return of the capital invested by him and, secondly, by the fact that he is responsible for the affairs of the company not with all his property, but only with capital, invested in shares. Shareholders at the general meeting elect the board, which manages all the affairs of the enterprise, the supervisory board and the audit commission, whose task is to control the activities of the board. Organizational work is carried out by hired directors, engineers, and so on. Shareholders, on the other hand, meet a certain number of times a year for board elections, hearing reports, distribution of income, etc.

The number of votes used by each meeting participant is determined by the number of shares he owns, while the number of shares that each shareholder can own is not limited. Each shareholder enjoys the right to sell his share at any time and thereby transfer the right to participate in the enterprise to another person. Every person who buys a share invests his money in the enterprise eventually. The holder of shares has the right to demand from the joint-stock company the return of the invested money only in the event of liquidation of the company.

However, even in this case, individual shareholders are often far from fully compensated. Thus, **the share is not so much the right to participate** in the enterprise as the right to receive income.

Despite this, each shareholder can return the money invested in the share at any time. To do this, he must sell his share on the securities market-stock exchange.

When issued, a share is sold at a strictly defined price, which is indicated on the share itself. This nominal price is equal to the value of the total capital of the joint-stock company divided by the number of issued shares. If, for example, the company's capital is 2,000,000 rubles, and the number of issued shares is 20,000, then the nominal price of each share should be 100 rubles.

A joint stock company does not have the right to issue its shares at a higher price, since in this case the security of the issued shares would not correspond to the obligations assumed by the joint stock company. However, when shares fall into the hands of individual holders and are brought to the market by them, no one can force sellers to charge a fixed price for a share and buyers to pay a fixed rate for shares.

On the stock exchange, each share acquires its own price, which does not remain unchanged, but constantly fluctuates depending on a number of factors. The action differs from a certificate, a bill of exchange and other strictly credit obligations, first of all, in that these credit obligations are fully repaid within a certain period. These documents are thus a certificate of the right to receive the values invested in them. The action, in its essence, is a document of unlimited duration. Its holder has no right to demand from the joint-stock company the return of the values invested by him in the joint-stock company. Even in the event of liquidation of a company, shareholders do not always receive full compensation. Thus, the share is only a certificate for the rights to the received income. It is clear that the higher the income generated by a share, the higher the share should be valued on the stock exchange. Depending on the fluctuation of the dividend brought by the share, its price also fluctuates.

In a capitalist company, any amount of money is converted into capital, acquires the ability to generate income. The capitalist puts his money in the bank, not so much to keep it (he could do this at home), but to get income. Giving his money to the banker, he, as it were, buys the right to receive income. True, it is also important for him that his money be preserved so that he can, if necessary, get it back in his hands.

In order to receive 5 rubles of annual income from the bank, the capitalist needs to invest, say, 100 rubles; in order to receive 50 rubles of income, 1,000 rubles must be invested, etc. Let us assume that a share brings its holder 7½ rubles in dividend. How much should it cost?

It is clear that the capitalist can receive such income from the bank only if he invests 150 rubles in the bank. Therefore, the share should cost the same. However, by giving his money to the bank, the capitalist can be absolutely sure of their complete safety; investing his money in a share, the capitalist always runs the risk of losing part of it if the income from the shares decreases somewhat and the share price falls. Therefore, he can regard the share slightly below 150 rubles. Let's say 130 rubles.

13

However, on average, the share price is determined, on the one hand, by its profitability and, on the other hand, by the level of interest on loans.

The following table fully confirms the idea expressed in production in the form of industrial capital. As in other industrial enterprises, they turn directly to the exploitation of labor and bring in the income usual for industrial enterprises (in our example - 80 / u) - Meanwhile, for individual shareholders, the purchase of shares is one type of credit transaction shares, they can at any time return the capital invested in shares in cash. Therefore, shareholders willingly agree to a rate of return that is only slightly higher than the loan interest.

In our example, the shareholders paid 3,000,000 rubles for all shares. With a loan interest rate of 5%, they should receive 150,000 rubles for this capital. annual income. If they receive not 150,000 rubles. income, and 160,000 rubles, they will rightly consider that they have done a very profitable business. Meanwhile, in order to be able to pay this amount to the shareholders, it is enough for a joint-stock company to invest in production not all of the capital raised, but only 2 million rubles, since the rate of industrial profit is higher than the level of interest on loans.

It is this circumstance that makes it possible for the bank issuing shares to pocket 1,000,000 rubles as founder's profit.

The market value of all shares admitted to the stock exchange during the decade 1904-1913 in Germany amounted to 5,704.4 million marks, while their nominal value was only 3,254.1 million marks. This means that of all the sums collected from individual shareholders, only 57%, or slightly more than half, ended up in production. The remaining 43%, or 450.3 million marks, stuck to the banks in the form of founders' profits.

Shares paid an average of 8.1% dividend, which amounted to 263.6 million marks.

Thus, the shareholders who actually paid for the shares 5.704.4 mil. marks, received 4.60 / about income, i.e. normal credit income. Just as the price of a share is a capitalized dividend, founder's profit is the capitalized difference between dividend and interest. In order to determine the founder's profit brought by one share of 100 Markov values, it is enough to subtract the loan interest from the dividend, divide the resulting difference by the loan interest and multiply by 100,

In our example:

$$\frac{(8.1 - 4.6)\ 100}{6.4\quad 4.6} = \frac{350}{4.6} = 76,08696$$

(...)

In order to be able to receive the founders' profit annually, the founders divide all shares into two groups - into ordinary (or ordinary) and privileged ones.

Preferred shares are distributed among mere mortals. They bring more or less solid income (on average, equal to the loan interest) and do not give voting rights to their owners.

Ordinary shares, which grant the right to vote to their owners, remain in the hands of the founders, who receive, although fluctuating, but extremely high income, including both dividend and founder's profit. Sometimes a clause is introduced into the charter of joint-stock companies that grants the pre-emptive right to vote at general meetings to holders of preferred shares.

In this case, preferred shares are transformed from the property of ordinary shareholders into the monopoly property of a group of the company's biggest bosses, who manage the company, using all the benefits of disposing of large capital. It is clear that in this case preferred shares are not at all what they are in the first case. In general, the methods of extracting founders' profits are extremely numerous and varied. They vary from country to country and from case to case.

However, no method of organizing joint-stock companies eliminates the possibility of extracting huge founders' profits. This opportunity in itself is a powerful stimulus for joint-stock companies and is no small factor contributing to the frenzied growth in the number of joint-stock enterprises at the expense of individual ones.

## Issue of bonds.

The mass of profits received by joint-stock companies and, first of all, the mass of founders' profits can be significantly increased by issuing bonds. These latter should not be confused with stocks.

While a share is a perpetual document and represents a certificate of the right to receive a certain share of the profits of a joint-stock company, a bond is a credit and only a credit document: bonds are obligatory to pay off, and they are repaid within a certain period. Therefore, a bond is not only a certificate of the right to receive income, but also a receipt for a certain value. The level of the dividend brought by a share is determined by the amount of profit of the enterprises of the joint-stock company.

Therefore, the dividend is constantly fluctuating with the rate of profit. A bond, on the other hand, brings a well-defined fixed income.

In connection with the fluctuations of the dividend, the rate of shares is constantly changing. On the other hand, a bond that brings a constant income is a valuable paper with a firm rate. A share gives its owner the right to vote at general meetings of shareholders, while the holder of the bond does not enjoy the right to vote. The issuance of the proclamations in no way alters the relationship with the strong general meetings. By issuing bonds, the tycoons of a joint-stock company increase the size of the social capital over which they dominate, but do not expand their contributions to company.

However, since joint-stock companies often direct the proceeds from the sale of bonds not to production, but to all sorts of speculative transactions, they often find themselves unable to pay bondholders the promised interest. Therefore, the legislation of most countries restricts the right of joint-stock companies to issue bonds.

In fact, of course, this is not the case. Each shareholder can exercise the right to vote, but the number of votes he has depends on how many shares he has in his pocket. Therefore, the affairs of a joint-stock company are decided not by all shareholders, but only by a handful of the most important shareholders. If any of the shareholders holds in his portfolio 51% of all shares issued by the company, he can dictate his will to the general meeting in the most unceremonious way: appoint at his own discretion a supervisory board, board, audit commission, administrative staff, distribute profits, etc. Petty investors, seeing that things are decided without them, in addition to them and against them, and not wanting to spend money on a trip, do not attend general meetings at all (for example, out of 40,000 shareholders of the famous Deutsche Bank usually no more than 40-50 people, i.e., 0.1%, while for each of those who appeared, on average, 500,000 marks of shares fell). Those of the small shareholders who attend general meetings usually do not dare to oppose the big bosses of company out of understandable "respect" for the people on whom their fate depends.

As a result, the number of shares that a capitalist who wants to dominate a joint-stock company must own is significantly reduced. Experience shows that it is enough to own 30-40% of all shares (1/3) in order to manage a stock company without hindrance.

In fact, a big capitalist who wants to dominate a joint-stock company does not even need to own its shares actually permanently. It is only necessary by the time of the next meeting of shareholders to concentrate in their hands a fairly solid "package" of shares. The technique of the matter is approximately as follows: at the general meeting of shareholders, one or another influential group of capitalists presents a number of shares sufficient to acquire a majority of votes. Using the majority of votes, it completely exercises its will at the meeting and gets the opportunity to appoint members of supervisory boards, directors, etc. at its own discretion. Having thus secured its influence in the company for a year, the management group often sells its shares, and the proceeds sales money throws at the conquest of other companies and businesses. However, by the next meeting of shareholders, he again acquires shares in company, again consolidates his influence in it, etc.

It is not surprising that, in this state of affairs, joint-stock companies are wholly and completely transformed into an instrument of the big capitalists, into a means of subordinating small capitals to large ones. Even the largest joint-stock companies, handling millions, as a rule fall under the control of even more powerful groups of capitalists.

The joint-stock form of organization of enterprises, therefore, **not only does not make capital the property of the whole people,** as people believe, but directly, on the contrary, is the tool with which the **big capitalists create the opportunity for**

**themselves** to dispose of not only their own capital, but also huge capital owned by small owners.

The system of <subsidiaries> enterprises.

With the dominance of the joint-stock form of enterprises, big capital acquires the ability to subjugate smaller capitals. Every accumulation of money-capital draws to itself and subjugates small capitals.

Let us suppose that a certain capitalist, who owns a capital of 700,000 rubles, uses his money to seize the shares of a certain company, which has a share capital of 2,000,000 rubles. The amount belonging to him is enough to buy up 35¾ of all the shares of the company. Having captured 1/J of all the shares, our capitalist becomes the complete owner at the general meetings of shareholders. This gives him the opportunity to place his own people at the head of the company and to dispose of the social capital of 2,000,000 rubles completely unhindered. If a joint-stock company, in addition to shares, also issues bonds worth, say, 1,000,000 rubles, our capitalist will have at his disposal a considerable social capital of 3000,000 rubles. We have already seen that there is no need for our capitalist to keep his money permanently in the shares of a given company. In the interval between two general meetings of shareholders, he can sell his shares and use the proceeds to buy shares in some other shareholder company. Let us suppose that in this way he manages to subdue another joint-stock company with a share capital of 1,500,000 rubles.

in this case, owning a capital of 700,000 rubles, our capitalist disposes of a social capital of 4,500,000 rubles. The social capital at the disposal of our capitalist exceeds his own capital by 6-1/2 times. However, that's not all. Let us imagine that the "subsidiary" companies subordinate to our capitalist invest in production not all the capital belonging to them, but only 2/3 of it, i.e. 3.000.000 rubles. The remaining 1,500,000 rubles they spend on the purchase of shares in other joint-stock companies.

An amount of one and a half million rubles is enough to seize 1/3 of the shares of several joint-stock companies with a capital of 4,500,000 rubles. These companies turn out to be completely subjugated and turn into the (grandchildren) companies of our capitalist. If, in addition to the share capital, these grand companies also have a capital of 3,000,000 rubles from the issue of bonds, we will have the following dependency ladder. A capital of 700,000 rubles subordinates to itself another, larger capital of 4,500,000 rubles, and this, in turn, subordinates an enormous capital of 7,500,000 rubles. Our capitalist, who has a comparatively insignificant sum of money, acquires the possibility of disposing of a huge capital of 12,000,000 rubles.

## NEW ROLE OF BANKS

**Banks as organizational centers of industry.**

The largest accumulations of money capital in capitalist company are formed in banks. Banks in the capitalist system are, literally, reservoirs of **free money capital**.

This is where all the money capital of modern company is poured, regardless of whether it is credit capital for its intended purpose or whether it is temporarily released from production.

From here all the capitalists who are in need of money draw the capital they need.

The entire free public money capital passes through the hands of the banks, which they distribute among the individual capitalists.

Just pointing to this fact is enough to understand that in a modern company where the dominant form of enterprise is the joint-stock company, banks should play an exceptional role. Let's stop, one1<0, on this issue in more detail.

The money flowing into the bank does not go to its permanent use. All deposits are made for a very specific period. By these terms, the bank is bound hand and foot in the matter of using the capital at its disposal.

He cannot invest them in organizing an industrial or commercial enterprise, because that would mean fixing the capital entrusted to him for a long time in business and depriving himself of the opportunity to pay off his obligations on time. Prior to the widespread distribution of the network of joint-stock companies, **the only field of activity of banking capital is, therefore, credit.**

At the same time, it is important to note that the main attention of banks is directed to short-term credit (under working capital) and trade credit, which do not require long-term capital investment.

The process of mobilizing capital, the process of wide development and expansion of joint-stock companies, creates a new favorite field of activity for banks.

The purchase of shares proves for banks in many way are more profitable operation than purely credit operations.

1) The capital spent on the purchase of shares is invested into action without a time limit.

At any time, at its first request, the bank can sell the shares and receive the money necessary to pay off creditors.

2) Due to the fact that the bank always has significant amounts of money at its disposal, it has the ability to buy a significant number of shares and dominate a number of joint-stock companies, thereby securing for itself a large credit market.

3) A large accumulation of money capital in the bank's cash desks makes it possible not only to buy up shares of already existing joint-stock companies, but also to organize new ones. Banks take over the issuance of shares and thereby ensure the receipt of both dividends and founders' profits.

4) Having a large number of shares, banks are able to regulate their prices on the stock exchange and, thanks to this, stock exchange speculation without any risk.

Thus, the **bank's income is replenished with still high stock exchange profit**. As a result of the listed advantages of joint-stock business over credit, **banks are investing an increasing part of their capital in industry.**

(statistical data)

If banks used to be exclusively credit institutions. However, now, as a result of the mobilization of capital, they are increasingly overgrown with industrial enterprises that depend on them and are subordinate to them, they are becoming more and more organizing centers of industry, and more and more are turning into commanding nodes of impersonal social capital.

The great interest of banks in the joint-stock business pushes them to master the entire "ladder of subordination" of the mobilized capital. The large accumulation of money-capital in their hands helps them to realize this striving for dominance over corporatized industry.

At the present time, every bank of any size dominates a number of joint-stock companies, keeps dozens of joint-stock enterprises belonging to the most diverse branches of production, dependent on it.

The power of the bank extends simultaneously to the railway company and to the editorial office of an influential newspaper, to a mining enterprise and to an advertising establishment. In all enterprises that are financially subordinate to it, the bank promotes "its own people" to senior positions.

Thus, he strengthens his connection with the joint-stock companies subordinate to him, through the so-called "private (or personal) union."

"The six largest Berlin banks were represented through their directors in 344 industrial companies and through their board members in another 407, in total in 751 companies .. In 289 companies, they had either two members of the supervisory boards or seats of their chairmen.

Among these commercial and industrial companies, we find the most diverse branches of industry: insurance business, communications, restaurants, theaters, the art industry, etc. On the other hand, on the supervisory boards of the same six banks was (in 1910 .) 51 major industrialists, including the director of the Krupp firm, the giant steamship company Hapag (Hamburg-Amerika), etc., each of the six banks from 1895 to many hundreds of industrial companies, namely from 281 to 419.

"According to the latest data book of 1909, there are 12,000 directors and members of councils in the management bodies of industrial companies in Germany, but 2,917 seats, 197 persons occupy the councils.

The record was broken by r Karl Fürstenberg of the Berliner Handelsgesellschaft with 44 mandates; Evgeny Dutman from Dresdener Bank occupies 35 seats. In general, of the various professions represented in the composition of the councils, the banking profession is most strongly represented, and therefore the greatest part-time job falls to its lot.

The same is true in the States of North America. The famous banking firm of Morgan in 1906 was represented in 109 enterprises. Among these enterprises there were 5 banks, 50 railways, 3 shipping companies, 8 trusted companies, 8 insurance companies, 40 industrial enterprises, etc.

One can judge what a huge role participation in joint-stock companies plays in the operations of German banks, if only by the fact that Deutsche Bank receives 10% of its entire profit from participation in industry, Darmstiidter Bank - 15-1 / 2% and "Berliner Handelsgesellschaft" -18%.

**Banking Concerns** *(Merged Business Groups).*

The banks themselves, which need huge capitals for their foundation, in turn, are built on joint-stock principles, they themselves represent joint-stock companies. This allows the most powerful banks to subjugate smaller banks with all credit, industrial and other enterprises associated with them. It often happens that a bank that controls a significant number of enterprises itself falls under the influence of a larger bank and finds itself in the position of a "subsidiary" or even "grandchild" enterprise.

On the eve of the war, the firm "I. I. Morgan and Co. itself controlled enterprises with a capital of 22½ billion dollars, which at that time amounted to 1/3 of the national property of the States. Closely connected with the firm were 18 other enterprises, together with which it subordinated to its influence a capital of 40 billion in the most diverse branches of the national economy, including 15.8 billion in industrial enterprises, 17.3 billion in railways, 4 billion in banks and other financial enterprises, 1-1/2 billion in mining and oil enterprises. The gigantic steel trust of the United States, the famous "United States Steel Corporation" with its 300,000 workers and employees, is Morgan's enterprise.

In the United States, 89 individuals hold over 2,000 directorships in various industrial, transportation, and other companies, with Morgan and Rockefeller directly or indirectly controlling almost all of these enterprises. Among the banks within the sphere of influence of the Morgan group are the two largest French banks (Credit Lyonnaise and Union Parisien), as well as the large English bank Schroeder.

Most recently (at the end of 1924), the Morgan Group, together with the Schroeder Bank, through the International Corporation for the Financing of Continental Industry organized by them, acquired 1.3 shares of the reorganized Deutsche Bank the business of this bank will go well, to acquire an additional number of its shares. Deutsche Bank thus became almost entirely a "subsidiary" of Morgan. However, Deutsche Bank itself is an organization that has not only subsidiaries, but even grandchildren and great-granddaughter companies.

Before the war, Deutsche Bank was a permanent participant in 17 other · banks, which were thus its "subsidiaries". These 17 "subsidiary" banks, in turn, participated in 34 "grandchildren" banks, and "grandchildren" banks have 7 "great grandchildren". In addition, the German Bank participated "for an unknown time" and "FROM time to time" in 13 banks, of which 5, in turn, participated in 14 banks, and 2 of these 14 dominate in 2 more .

In total, the sphere of influence of the German Bank included 87 banks, among which there were large foreign firms (for example, Vienna Banking Union, Siberian Trade Bank, Russian Bank for Foreign Trade, Accounting Bank, Petersburg International Bank "and many others).

Each of the banks included in the group, of course, controls a huge number of industrial and commercial, transport, insurance companies and, thus, the dominance of the "Deutsche Bank" over a number of banks provides it with the opportunity to manage not only enterprises directly related to it, but also by all enterprises subordinate to its "subsidiaries", "great-grandchildren", and "great-grandchildren" banks.

All enterprises dependent on the same bank form a banking group. A banking group can be depicted using the following diagram.

The banking concern includes not only joint-stock companies, but also individual enterprises. There are enough funds in the hands of the banks to subdue them.

Every capitalist needs money from time to time. He receives this money from the bank. If it is more or less easy to get a short-term loan from a bank (a loan against working capital), then a loan against fixed capital is much more difficult. Giving money for a long time, the bank always. runs the risk of losing them if the position of the enterprise is shaken during this time.

Therefore, the bank, issuing a loan for fixed capital, sets the debtor a number of conditions. The debtor must allow permanent control over his enterprise. The debtor is obliged not to resort to the help of other banks and henceforth to be credited only in the bank that gave him the loan. The debtor undertakes to comply with the directives of the bank in the field of trade policy and coordinate its actions with the actions of enterprises subordinate to the bank, etc.

Credit is a powerful tool with which the bank brings individual industrial enterprises into subjection.

Thus, **not only joint-stock companies, but also individual enterprises become dependent on banks**.

At the present time **it is difficult to find even a tiny little shop that,** in one way or another, directly or indirectly, **would not depend on this or that bank** and would not obey its directives in its trading activities.

## Concentration of Banks.

Along with the change in the scope of banks, the nature of competition between them also changes. In the past, banks only clashed with each other in the area of credit. Now, however, when banking capital is strongly interested in the affairs of industry, when the profits of each bank depend on the state of affairs of the enterprises associated with it, every collision of two industrial enterprises leads to a collision of banks interested in their affairs.

Banks have now turned from only credit institutions into credit, industrial, and commercial institutions at the same time, and, accordingly, the struggle between banking concerns is carried out simultaneously in all areas of capital investment. In all places where capital is invested, in which the bank is "interested", it can be hit equally hard. The bank suffers both if it is deprived of credit links and if the enterprises associated with it go bankrupt. For each bank, the front of the struggle expands, lengthens. Now, for a successful struggle, the bank needs to have exceptionally large capitals, for it must itself defend itself against the pressing enemy and support its "offspring" ("subsidiaries" and "grandchildren" enterprises) with capital and expand its influence, capturing more and more new enterprises.

Therefore, the last decades have been marked by a rapid increase in concentration in the field of banking.

The situation is somewhat different in Germany. Here, one can speak of a reduction in the absolute number of banks only as applied to Berlin. In Berlin in 1895 there were 16 banks, in 1900 - 18, and in 1912 - only 9. In the provinces, the number of banks, under the influence of the feverish industrial development of Germany, even grew. However, this does not mean, of course, that there was no concentration of bank capital. The size of the average bank increased.

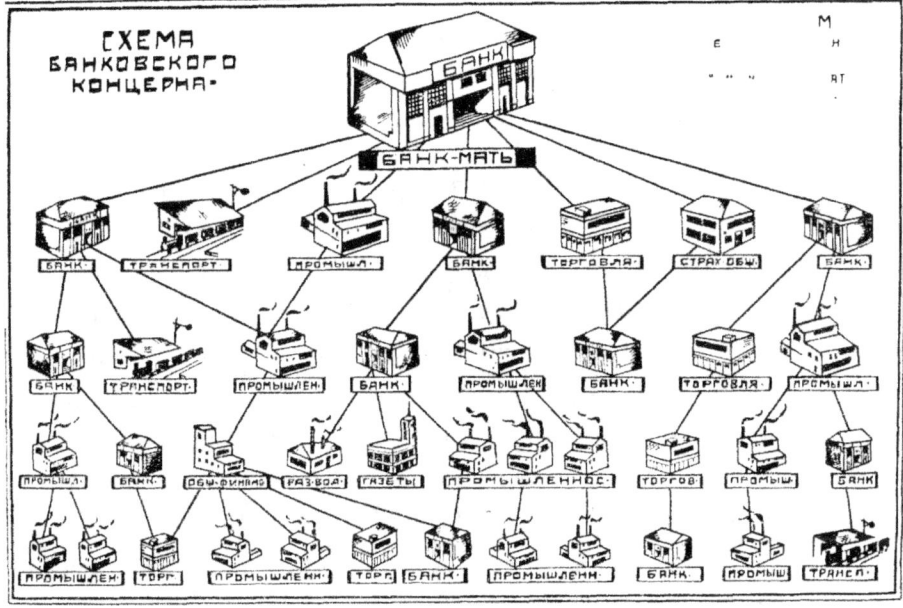

(statistical data)

The process of concentration of bank capital in Russia was carried out in a similar way.

Of the several dozen banks that exist in each country, not all reach the same size. The bulk of banking capital is concentrated in a few of the largest banks, which thus dominate both the credit market and all branches of the national economy.

The rest of the banks play a secondary role, are on the way to death and, in most cases, are completely dependent on one or another large bank.

In 1914, the capital of 47 Russian banks amounted to 584.9 million rubles; 62.3% of all this capital - 364.5 million. rubles were in the hands of 1 7 St. Petersburg banks.

The same picture in Germany. In 1912 the capital of all credit banks in Germany amounted to 2.963 million marks. More than "3/5 of this capital (1.250 million marks) belonged to the 9 largest banks (Berlinsl (them), while the share of the remaining 147 banks accounted for less than 3/5.

The capital of each of the 9 largest banks reached, on average, 139 million. marks, while the average capital of each of the rest did not even reach 12 million. stamps; The 9 largest banks play almost the same role in the economic life of the country as the 147 others. This is worth thinking about. The picture becomes even more striking if we remember that **of the 147 banks mentioned, a good half are nothing more than "subsidiaries" of the largest banks.** That this estimated figure is not exaggerated is proved by the fact that already in 1911 6 of these banks "permanently participated" in 63 German banks, and the sphere of influence of Deutsche Bank alone included 87 large and small banks.

*(statistical data)*

France is dominated by only 4 major banks. "Their position is so predominant that they determine the functions of all other banks, presenting them with a field for the full application of labor only where, due to their internal structure, they could not take an active part. They cover the whole country with their network of branch offices, through which they are able to absorb a significant, if not most, part of the **free money capital.**

**Merging industrial capital with credit.**

Things should not be conceived in such a way that, to the extent that industrial enterprises are subordinated to banks, industrial capital is subordinated to credit capital.

**This is precisely the essence of modern (financial) capitalism**, that banks act here, not only as representatives of credit capital, but as representatives of both credit and industrial capital at the same time. The following illustration will make the statement more understandable:

"In the late 1860s and early 1870s, the Standard Oil Company began operations, at first with a capital of $1 million, which by 1892 had increased to millions of dollars. Thanks to huge profits, in the hands of leaders; The aforementioned company accumulated a large cash capital, which already in 1886 exceeded 17 million dollars.

Rockefeller and his associates chose National City Bank as their main base. The choice was successful. Not being particularly large, this bank gained fame for itself

Rockefeller and his associates chose National City Bank as their main base. The choice was successful. Not being particularly large, this bank gained fame for its cautious, non-speculative policy, and enjoyed the full confidence of the public ... The merger was beneficial to both parties.

Banking capital greatly increased the cash of the Stadart Oil Company, which it needed to develop the business and various financial transactions.

The bank, with the help of millions of capitals of the Standard Oil Company, was able to expand its activities to a grand scale ... The bank annexed a number of other banks. The combined capitals and deposits of all these banks reach $700 million.

It is not surprising that the bank becomes the main monetary center of the country and takes part in all more or less large transactions, whether it is the financing of industrial and other companies, the sale of various securities, and the like.

We see that **Rockefeller acts simultaneously as** head of **both credit and industrial capital.**

If he subjugates this or that industrial enterprise through the mediation of his bank, this, of course, will in no way indicate the subordination of industrial capital to credit capital, but will undoubtedly be a case of the subordination of small capital, regardless of the sphere of their application, to large capital, which is a synthesis of industrial and credit capital - stock or finance capital. Rockefeller is no exception, of course.

Another major financial king of the United States - **Morgan is at the same time the head of one of the largest banks in the world** - the National Bank of Commerce and a group of banks adjacent to it, which had a total capital of more than 600 million before the war. dollars. At the same time, **Morgan is the head of the largest "Steel Trust"** (United States Steel Corporation) and one of the largest railway kings (225 railways-4-7.206 miles of track).

**What kind of capital does Morgan represent** - industrial or credit? **Both taken together,** merged together, **represent finance capital.** The subordination of one-third of the entire economy of the United States to the Morgan Bank is, therefore, not the subordination of industrial capital to credit capital, but the subordination of small industrial and credit capital to big finance capital.

## Company for funding.

The main consequence of the mobilization of capital is not the subordination of industrial capital to credit, but the fusion of industrial capital with credit. Thanks to the mobilization of capital, any capital, regardless of the sphere of its application, takes the form of stock capital. Namely, as a result of this, the role of banks in modern company is increasing.

Always having large money capital ready for application, the banks can use this capital to buy up shares and, consequently, to subjugate social capital.

However, along with banks, other capitalist organizations can also acquire a decisive influence on social capital if they constantly have at their disposal a sufficient mass of capital in monetary or fund form.

Recently, the so-called "companies for financing" (companies for participation) have advanced to the forefront among these organizations, which successfully compete in spreading their influence with banks. While the organization of banks is entirely adapted to the production of credit operations, and their founding activity is only the result of the accumulation of large masses of social capital in the bank cash desks, "companies for financing" make founding activity their goal and create their entire organization in relation to this goal.

"Companies for financing" are usually established by industrialists in the form of joint-stock companies.

A group of capitalists, by issuing a large number of small shares, concentrates in their hands an enormous social capital, which they use entirely to buy up the shares of other joint-stock companies and subjugate industrial, commercial, credit and other enterprises to themselves.

The organization of companies for financing" allows the leaders of industry not only not to fall under the influence of banks, but, on the contrary, to independently subjugate both industrial enterprises and banks.

Concerns are created with the help of the establishment of "financial companies", which are not headed by banks, but directly by industrial companies.

A classic example of funding companies are the "participating companies" organized by the well-known German electrical trust "General Electricity Company" (A. E. G.).

In total, nine companies were organized by this trust for financing: the Bank of Electric Values in Berlin, the General Company of Local Railways and Trams in Berlin, Company for Electricity in Berlin, Bank for Electrical Enterprises in Zurich, Company for Electricity Enterprises in Berlin, Joint-Stock Company for Electricity (ex. W. Lahmeier & Co. in Frankfurt am Main, Joint Stock Company of Enterprises V. K. E., Joint Stock Company ElectroBank in Hamburg, Joint Stock Bank for Electrical Industry in Berlin.

All these companies are led by a trust. A. E. G. and those subordinate to him are organizations remarkably reminiscent of banks both in name and organization and in the nature of their operations. They, like banks, are engaged in the issue of shares and stock exchange speculation, and even perform a number of purely credit operations. However, they differ from banks, firstly, in that they are completely dependent on the industrial enterprise and are an instrument in its hands, and, secondly, in that the center of their operations is the financing of specially joint-stock companies and that it is precisely these operations adapted their apparatus.

The most powerful of all the listed companies is undoubtedly the Electricity Enterprise Bank in Zurich.

This "bank", being a "subsidiary" of A.E.G., in turn controls 7 funding companies in Switzerland, Italy, Belgium and France. In addition, he participates in 29 industrial joint-stock companies (power plants, trams, etc.) located in Germany (11), Italy (9), Switzerland (5), Spain and Portugal (3) and Poland (1).

The second giant "Company of Electrical Enterprises" runs 4 major "funding companies" in Belgium ("Belgian General Electricity Company}> . and "Finance Company for Transport and Industrial Enterprises"), in Italy ("Company for the Development of Electrical Enterprises in Italy") and Hungary ('-"Joint-stock company of electrical and transport enterprises").

Within Germany, it controls a long series of enterprises, among which there are several very large electrical, gas, transport, and tram companies. The "Electricity Company" in Berlin subjugates 90 different enterprises within Germany, most of which are created by itself, etc.

How large a role the "funding companies" play in subordinating social capital to the big industrial magnates is shown by the following table, characterizing the financial power of the "General Electricity Company" (see table p. 55).

*(statistical data)*

The capital subordinated to V.K.E. through the "companies for financing" significantly (almost 2 times) exceeds the equity capital of this gigantic enterprise.

The development and spread of "communities for financing" in itself causes significant damage to the so-called "dominance of the banks", however, it does not break the fusion of industrial capital with credit capital, it does not destroy financial capitalism. Similarly, the regrouping of economic forces in a number of countries, which took place during the last imperialist war and as a result of which the leadership of social capital once again passed into the hands of the industrialists, does not undermine the roots of finance capital.

During the imperialist war, large industrial enterprises (especially in heavy industry) received huge profits. At the same time, the profits of the banks increased comparatively less significantly, since the governments willingly financed the industry, not stopping even from printing an excess amount of paper money. In this way, huge amounts of money flowed into the hands of industrial enterprises, which they used to organize "companies for financing" and to directly buy up the shares of other enterprises.

In those countries where there was a significant depreciation of the currency, the benefits of using credit were added to these advantages. Large industrial enterprises, receiving loans in abundance from banks, returned them to the banks in paper currency. Since the exchange rate of money fell significantly during the time of the loan, industrial enterprises received the entire difference in the form of a premium for using the loan. Credit thus became a pump by which large industrial enterprises pumped capital from the cash registers of the banks to their own cash desks.

Especially in Germany, the enrichment and flourishing of industrial concerns was facilitated, paradoxically as it may seem, by the annexation and occupation of the most industrial areas of the country. For the enterprises taken by the French, German industrialists received large monetary compensation from the government. This gives them the opportunity to concentrate in their hands huge amounts of money, which they used to subjugate joint-stock companies at home and abroad.

The same thing happened during the occupation of the Ruhr, when the Ruhr industrialists received huge sums from the German government in the form of "compensation" for the temporary suspension of production during the period of "passive resistance". The essence of this process of regrouping of economic forces was quite clearly outlined by AV in his article "A New Phase in the Development of German Banking Capital".

"Along with other regroupings of economic forces in Germany during the period of inflation", he writes, "one of the most decisive for its further development is the regrouping and balance of forces between industrial and financial capital (it would be more correct to say, "industrial and banking". A.K.).

The information economy at first noticeably strengthened the position of the banks. The first years, until approximately the middle of 1922, are characterized by a significant increase in the issuing activity of banks. The depreciation of the mark caused in the ranks of industry and trade a continuous need for working capital. Numerous enterprises by that time were transformed into joint-stock companies in order to attract new capital. Banks, through which issues are made, not only derive significant income, but also increase their influence in the management and control of commercial and industrial enterprises by participating.

As the rate of depreciation of the brand accelerates, this dominance of the banks is on the wane. The leading commercial and industrial circles very quickly comprehend the secret of the inflationary mechanism. They learn to use the depreciation of the mark in the widest possible sizes, without resorting to the help of banks. By that time, the role of the stock exchange had reached extraordinary significance. The broadest segments of the population, in an effort to secure the remnants of their savings from depreciation, rush to all sorts of stock exchange values, which for the time being gave the illusion of "real values". In this state of affairs, the placement of new issues did not present any particular difficulties. By means of consortiums specially created for this purpose, the industry, bypassing the intermediary of banks, independently places its new issues, raking in the founder's profit, a significant share of which usually had to be ceded to bank capital.

In parallel, during the period of inflation in the balance sheets of banks, the proportion of other people's funds begins to decline more and more. Previously, banks' lending to trade and industry was carried out mainly at the expense of deposits, but now this source is rapidly drying up.

The circle of activity of banks is narrowing more and more. In their hands, mainly, remains a purely intermediary function in supplying clients with securities; they turn into not always the right authority for obtaining loans in paper marks from the Imperial Bank.

Very characteristic of the economy of the inflationary period was the widespread development of the so-called "group banks" (Konzernbanken).

Even before the war, there were frequent **cases when one or another large industrial association, in an effort to emancipate from the control of bank capital,** with which any significant financing from a large bank was inevitably connected, **created its own credit institutions.** Such a "concern" bank, in essence, already in pre-war times, was the large Berlin bank "Handelsgesellchaft", most closely associated with the "General Electricity Company" (A. E. G.). The large industrial associations of western Germany often succeeded in taking possession of rather significant 11 provincial banks. But, **in general, these facts remained isolated.**

Since the prominent banks of the provinces were losing their independence on a larger scale, these were cases where **they became dependent not on industrial capital,** but were taken over **by large metropolitan banks** and through the concentration of banking capital. During the period of inflation, the concentration of bank capital took place only in the first years. However, as inflation continued to develop, concentration in banking is suspended.

At the same time, provincial banks have to withstand vigorous pressure from the "new concerns". These gigantic associations of commercial and industrial enterprises, which have grown enormously during the period of war and inflation due to the unprecedented expropriation of the broad working masses, small rentiers, middle and small capital, are striving for complete independence from large banking institutions.

Most of these "concerns" either turn their financial departments into banking institutions, or which was much easier, buy up existing provincial banks, turning them into banks of their "concerns." If at first the establishment of these "concern banks" was aimed at saving on interest and commissions, then later they made it possible for concerns to quickly use their own and other people's working capital. Typical in this respect is the policy of the Stinnes concern, which, after an unsuccessful attempt to take over the Berlin bank "Handelsgesellschaft", takes over the largest provincial bank in Germany, "Barmer Bnnkverein".

This includes the penetration of the Michael concern into the Deutsche Vereinsbank and the less successful similar operations of the now collapsed Barmatov concern (Merkur-Bank and Preussische Hypothekeen-Actien bank).

The dominating position of the big banks was dealt an all the more severe blow because, during the period of inflation, the process of concentration of money capital gave way to extreme dissipation and the development of competition. In the last inflationary year of 1923, leaving aside the smaller banks, 99 joint-stock "general" banks were established throughout

Germany. Along with this, about 40 special industrial banks and the same number of agricultural banks were established during the same year. In their totality, these institutions diverted a significant part of the already reduced capital, which had previously been sent in a single, wide stream to the big banks. The fact is that during the period of inflation, large banks were not able, despite the extraordinary increase in personnel, to cope with the execution of stock exchange orders of their numerous clientele. For purely technical reasons, they should have given up on bringing in new customers...

*(statistical data)*

"The expropriation of broad strata of the middle and petty bourgeoisie in Germany as a result of inflation and the extremely slow rate of accumulation to which Germany is now doomed make it impossible to place on the internal German market new issues, JJ of which German industry needs to increase its working capital and trade. This circumstance will further lead to a weakening of the position of German banks in relation to industry. The personal union of banks with the largest industrial enterprises is already in many cases fictitious.

The hegemony of banking capital took the place of the economic leadership of a small group of people at the head of the overgrown concerns of heavy industry. '

## Industrial "Concerns." Stinnes "Concern".

As a result of the successful competition of special "companies for financing" with the usual universal banks, the so-called industrial concerns are becoming widespread. **Industrial concerns** differ from banking ones only in that they are not headed by banks, but by industrialists who have one or more companies as an instrument of their activity for financing. Such concerns appeared relatively recently (shortly before the war) and especially developed only in the post-war period. Namely, due to the short period of their development, industrial concerns have not yet had time to crystallize into any definite type. They sometimes cover enterprises in the most diverse and not directly related sectors of the economy (the Stinnes concern in Germany, Castiglioni in Austria, etc.), sometimes they focus on industries directly related to each other by the unity of the production process (General Electricity Company Concern, Krupp Concern, etc.). Depending on which of these two types of the concern belongs to, the nature of the relationship between the enterprises included in it, is also established.

So, in the Stinnes concern, the vast majority of enterprises were not connected between-connections "and" nothing but the unity of property, while in the General, they are approaching each other, in the activity as a whole, they are all closer to each other, their activity is linked by a single plan, and the whole concern, as a whole, is **increasingly approaching in type the American trust.**

However, what is characteristic of the process of "concernification" of the modern capitalist economy is not so much the formalized and outwardly visible production association of enterprises, but the establishment of an invisible financial connection between them, a connection built only on the association of property, but not the association of enterprises. A **classic example in** this respect is the notorious **Stinnes concern.**

By 1921 German-Luxembourg had: 12 own coal horses with a productivity (in 1919) of 3.05 mill. tons yrJ1Я and 854 thous. tons of coke, iron mines on the Ruhr, in the Zierland, in Nassau, on the Weser, in the Rhineland, in the Harz, near Kleinbremen.

Ore concessions in Oberfranken and Oberfalz, 9 ironworks and ironworks with 10 blast furnaces, 11 open-hearth furnaces, 21 puddling furnaces, 1 electric furnace. German-Luxembourg produced: coal, coke, cast iron, steel, steel casting, sheet iron, wire, tin, bridges, railroads. arrows, cars, locomotives and wagons, ships, agricultural machinery, etc. The number of workers in Germany-Luxemburg reached 47,000. By 1921 German-Luxembourg had: 12 own coal mines with a productivity (in 1919) of 3.05 mill tons annually and 854 thousand mill tons of coke, iron mines on the Ruhr, in the Zierland, in Nassau, on the Weser, in the Rhineland, in the Harz, near Kleinbremen. Ore concessions in Oberfranken and Oberfalz, 9 ironworks and ironworks with 10 blast furnaces, 11 open-hearth furnaces, 21 puddling furnaces, 1 electric furnace. German-Luxembourg produced: coal, coke, cast iron, steel, steel casting, sheet iron, wire, tin, bridges, railroads. arrows, cars, locomotives and wagons, ships, agricultural machinery, etc. The number of workers in Germany-Luxemburg reached 47,000.

*(statistical data)*

The axis of this concern, its core is the Joint Stock Company for Navigation and Overseas Trade "Hugo Stinnes." "This company is not only a manufacturing enterprise in the sense that it carries out independent trading operations and owns shipping lines leading to all parts of the world, it is also not a "company for financing". which concentrates in its portfolio participation in a number of diverse enterprises. The company was founded in 1917. Hugo Stinnes, his wife, Mrs. Stinnes, and StinnE's close associate, Thomas, sit on the Council of this company. Stinnes's son sits on the board of the island. The parent company is associated with a number of enterprises. of which the majority are funding companies. Through these companies, Stinnes subjugates a number of shipbuilding enterprises…

*(statistical data)*

Concentrating in his hands the nodes of Germany's water transport, Stinnes, however, does not confine himself to purely transport operations.

"The Joint Stock Company of Shipping and Overseas Trade Hugo Stinnes conducts export and import operations on a roma scale.

Close ties with the coal, ore, iron, electrical, engineering, shipbuilding and shipping industries put this society beyond all competition and gives eJ11y an almost monopoly position in German foreign trade. Foreign trade operations open up a wide influx of money capital into the hands of Stinnes in foreign currency and in gold. During the period of "gentle inflation" in Germany, this circumstance gave Stinnes special strength and made it easier for him to further spread his influence over German industry.

"The Joint Stock Company of Navigation and Overseas Trade Hugo Stinnes conducts export and import operations on a large scale. Close ties with the coal, ore, iron, electrical, engineering, shipbuilding and shipping industries put this society beyond all competition and gives it an almost monopoly position in German foreign trade. Foreign trade operations open up a wide influx of money capital into the hands of Stinnes in foreign currency and in gold. During the period of "gentle inflation" in Germany, this circumstance gave Stinnes **special strength and made it easier for him to further spread his influence** over German industry.

Not wanting to let the foreigners who come on the Stinnes steamer to Germany, and most importantly, the gold and foreign currency they bring, out of their hands, Stinnes started buying up hotels and chicken houses. For this purpose, together with Harag and other maritime societies, in 1919 he organised, in 1919, the organ of the Hamburg Relationships, in which Stinnes held decisive influence. Within a few months this company has bought dozens of the best hotels in various places in Germany and also abroad. Such gigantic enterprises as the Esplanade Hotel in Berlin, the Atlantic Hotel in Hamburg, etc., fell into his hands.

By acquiring the largest hotels frequented by a diverse public, Stinnes pursued a specific goal. A foreign traveler can, while still on a ship, book a hotel room with the same society in almost any major city… And this is now very important: the currency that a foreigner brings usually remains in the hands of Stinnes.

This method of combining production is extremely characteristic of Stinnes. Namely, the desire to add to the branches of production in which he already dominates, other branches connected with them commercially or technically, led Stinnes in his concentration activity.

So, as a result of the war, it turned out to be very difficult to supply mines and mines with fastening timber.

In order to supply his own or associated enterprises with this necessary commodity, Stinnes bought up a large number of forests in East Prussia and other parts of Germany.

However, the supply of coal-mining enterprises with fixed logs could not serve as a basis for the sufficient use of the forests belonging to him. In order to fully exploit the benefits of forestry, Stinnes bought a number of sawmills, woodworkers, furniture, and pulp companies. Pulp production entailed the purchase of paper mills. Printing houses followed the paper mills, newspapers and publishing houses followed, followed by telegraph agencies, and so on. In the hands of Stinnes were from 70 to 100 newspapers of the most diverse political trend in Germany and Austria…

(statistical data)

Stinnes also controls the "Ala" announcement society, which supplies newspapers with advertisements. Anyone who knows what role advertisements play in the life of a modern newspaper will realize what a powerful means of pressure on the press this agency is.

Similarly, Stinnes became the oil king. As owner of a huge merchant fleet, Stinnes felt an urgent need for petroleum fuel. On the other hand, oil in the German and European markets competed with coal supplied by Stinnes enterprises and coal processing products. This prompted Stinnes to come to grips with oil. Stinnes buys the vast majority of the filling stations scattered along the German coast from private individuals and monopolizes this business in his own hands.

*(statistical data)*

Transport and distribution of products is in the hands of its own commercial enterprises and a number of subordinates. One of the largest consumers of products are the rest of Stinnes' concerns. The concern is subordinated to Akts. The island of Hansa, which owns a large amount of oil-bearing land in Hanover and carries out extensive drilling work in this province. Together with the company "Benz" Stinnes, Riebeck "organized a company for the sale of mineral oil.

The Stinnes-Riebeck concern is indirectly associated with Rockefeller Standard Oil, participating with it in the German-Ameoican Oil Company and with the Anglo-Dutch oil trust Royal Dutch, which takes part in Api. In addition, "Stinnes-Riebeck" participates in the "International Petroleum Society" in Rotterdam and uncontrollably disposes of the "Danish Joint Stock Company" for the import of oil and gasoline.

Let us dwell only on the inclusion of large banks in the Stinnes concern.

In the summer of 1922, Stinnes managed to concentrate in his hands 36% of the shares of the already repeatedly mentioned Berliner Häpdelsgesellschaft bank.

This largest bank, which is one of the 7 leading banks in Germany, thus fell under the influence of Stinnes and admitted two of his representatives to its Supervisory Board.

The importance of subordinating this bank to Stinnes can be seen if only from the fact that until then the Berliner Hädelsgesel!schaft had been closely connected with the competing concern of the General Electricity Company and conducted all its affairs. In 1923, Stinnes seized the majority of the shares of the large provincial bank Barmener Banküerein, which has 135 branches, and completely subordinated its operations to his interests; after that he brought this bank under the control of HädelsgeseJlschaft'y and thus created an enormous reservoir of capital for his operations. In addition, Stinnes is closely associated with the two largest Berlin banks, DiscontogeseJlschaft and Darmstadter Bank, and with a number of Austrian, Hungarian, Italian, and Swiss banks.

The scope of activities of the Stinnes concern is not limited to the state borders of Germany. In Austria and Hungary, Poland and Czecho-Slavakia, Romania, Turkey, Yugoslavia and Bulgaria, Italy, Switzerland, Holland, Denmark, Sweden and even England, there are scattered enterprises that are directly or indirectly dependent on Stinnes or are branches of enterprises included in his concerns.

After the death of Hugo Stinnes (April 1924), the actual heirs of all his vast property were his two sons Edmund and Hugo Stinnes. At first they tried to continue the policy of their father. In 1924, they bought the AGA automobile company (AG för Automobilbau) and merged it with the Dinoswerke automobile company, which had previously been part of their concern.

They acquire the Marentheim Spa Joint-Stock Company, several hotels in München and the Nassauer Hof Hotel in Wiesbaden.

They take part in the Elberfeld Society of Copper and Brass Works and in the Cologne Society of Koasok — Franz Raskin,,. They subjugate Alfred Urbigend's ironworks in Munich and Akts. About the wire industry of Tenis. They take over the Dollburn Oil Refinery Society in Halle. They acquire part of the shares of the O-Rhine coal mines and briquette factories. The eldest of the brothers (Edmund) establishes a large cinematographic enterprise, Westfilm, etc. A closer relationship is established between the Rhine-Elbe-SchuckFlika Kert-Union concern, on the one hand, and the ironworks of Friedrich Charlotenburg, on the other. At the same time, the Stinnes brothers do not "commonly weaken the nature of their expansion abroad, They capture the Austrian mineral products, asphalt and chemical industries of Brem", establish coal trading companies in England (Edinburgh), enterprises seize a controlling stake in the Romanian oil company de Petrole,,, organize jointly with German and Dutch firms an enterprise for the production of soda, soap and castor oil in Holland, conclude an agreement with Gapag (Hamburg-America Linien) and North German Lloyd on the regulation of freight traffic on the South American line and cooperation in the field of passenger traffic, etc. Altogether, our guests at StinStinnes have acquired about 80 new enterprises. However, the young Stabilines had to work in extremely unfavorable conditions. On the one hand, the formation of the German mark deprived the Stinnes concerns of an influx of purely speculative profits and, on the other hand, knocked out of their hands the great advantage that was in the conditions of inflation the possession of foreign currency. At the same time, the general normalization of economic life in Germany, which followed the adoption of the Dawes Plan, eliminated the shortage of raw materials on which the rise of large coal and ore firms was based. The influx of foreign capital again filled the cash desks of banks and increased their share in economic life.

Under these conditions, the Stinnes concern encountered, on the one hand, difficulties in the field of financing the diversified enterprises included in it, recruited into the concern without any clause and system, and, on the other hand, met with centrifugal tendencies on the part of these enterprises, which the concern now could no longer provide the former advantages.

Having made several attempts to create a closer production relationship between its constituent enterprises and to free itself from unnecessary prejudices, the Stinnes concern became entangled in financial difficulties and crumbled into its component parts (in June 1925). Actually, only Stinnes' personal concern was finally destroyed. As for the main components of "SiemensRhein-Elba-Schuckert-Union", they have survived and are now included in new grandiose combinations.

The Stinnes concern collapsed, in large measure, because the growth of ero was built entirely on the use of painful processes of the economy, and not on its development. As soon as these painful processes stopped and partly stopped, the Stinnes concern lost the strength to grow. However, the Stinnes concern more clearly revealed in its development those forms of concentration of the capitalist economy that are by no means the product of only post-war devastation. This type of concentration is still present in most European countries. A number of concerns that managed in time to take measures to get rid of superfluous enterprises, the management of which turned out to be unbearable for them, and to establish production links between their constituent enterprises, have survived in Germany to this day. Such are the General

Electricity Company, Krupp, Thyssen, Stumm, Wolff, l'aniel, Mikael, and others. Concerns of this type also exist in other countries. Such are the concerns of Leverhelm (the Lever brothers), Armstrong and Vickers in England, the concerns of Schneider-Kroes and Luscher in France, Kreller in Holland, etc.

The **main significance of industrial concerns** lies in the fact that they link fragmented enterprises into single powerful sheaves and thereby **accelerate the development of the principles of organization in a capitalist economy.**

## CAPITALIST MONOPOLY

**Syndicates, cartels, trusts, capitalist monopolies.**

Industrial concerns represent a relatively new form of organization of production. Moreover, this form of capitalist associations is not yet equally widespread in all countries of the capitalist world. Even if the industrial concern cannot be regarded as a specifically German form of capitalist association, as some scholars do, it must nevertheless be admitted that this form of organization of production has acquired decisive importance so far only in Europe, and mainly in Germany.

Financial-capitalist practice, however, long before the war worked out a whole series of methods for organizing industrial monopolies. Provided that the vast majority of capital employed in industry, trade v. transport is linked around single centers (banks or "funding societies"), the process of concentration of banks (or "funding societies") is, at the same time, a process of concentration of social capital.

When some enterprises leading the concerns are subordinated to others, together with the vanquished, the entire branch of the national economy dependent on him, the entire concern of the vanquished, is an integral part of the winner's concern. The management of social capital is concentrated in fewer and fewer hands. Along with this comes the centralization of production.

Each center "interested" in industrial affairs strives, of course, to ensure that the enterprises adjacent to it do not compete with each other, do not cause damage to each other. Using his influence on the enterprises dependent on him, he forces them to merge.

Capitalist associations are of the most varied types. They differ from each other both in the term of the agreement between enterprises, and in the strength of the connection between them, and in the number of branches of economic activity they seize.

The first stage of capitalist associations are short-term agreements between several large entrepreneurs regarding prices (rings, corners). This type of agreement is usually concluded between the largest exchange tycoons for one successful speculation. Now, after the end of the operation, such agreements fall apart.

A higher level of capitalist unity is the cartel. Here agreements are established not for a short period, but sometimes even for several years, and, at the end of the term of the agreement, the agreements are often renewed.

A cartel usually unites a fairly large number of industrial enterprises. Cartel members set mandatory minimum prices for their products and maximum wages, distribute distribution areas among both, and elect a board that monitors the fulfillment of the terms of the agreement by individual members and guides them in the fight against entrepreneurs who have not joined the cartel.

The **cartel is built** not only on voluntary, but, to a large extent, on coercive principles. With its huge capital and unlimited support from 6anCoR, the cartel has the ability to "put pressure" on enterprises that do not want to join it, and thus causes great damage to the "wild" (independent) entrepreneur. The cartel deprives him of his credit by buying up the raw materials needed by the "savage", enters into an agreement with railways and steamship companies that refuse to transport the goods of the "savage", deprives him of his labor force through agreements with workers' unions, etc. Most of the "wild" cannot endure this unbearable struggle and join the cartel against their will. Using such powerful means, cartels

51

often achieve a monopoly position in the country, seizing entire branches of production.

An even higher form of association is the **syndicate.** In this case, cartel members not only set mandatory prices, but also organize joint sales of goods. For this purpose, a special enterprise is based on joint-stock principles - a syndicate, which buys their goods from all participants and delivers these goods to the consumer monopoly, without competitors. The shares of this enterprise are distributed among the parties to the agreement. The category of syndicates also includes more complex organizations, known as "pools".

These "pools" ("common cauldron") have a common cash register, where the profit of all participants arrives, which is then distributed among them in a certain proportion, pre-established depending on the size of production and the share of each of the pool participants.

In relation to the "wild" syndicates use the same means as the cartels. Just like cartels, they often achieve a monopoly in production. However, syndicates (and especially pools) differ from cartels in much greater stability and strength. If the cartel only controls the fulfillment of the terms of the agreement by individual participants, then the syndicate prevents the participants from violating these conditions. **In a cartel**, each participant often violates the agreement and thereby **creates the ground for conflicts between the capitalis**ts who have entered into the agreement.

In a syndicate, all participants are deprived of the opportunity to violate the concluded agreement. However, the highest degree of capitalist association is undoubtedly the American-type trust. The private traders of the trust simply merge their enterprises into a single enterprise. Each of the capitalists belonging to the trust transfers his enterprises to the trust and receives in return a corresponding number of shares in the trust. The trust is thus a private joint-stock company whose shares are distributed among the owners of the enterprises included in it.

**Both the cartel and the syndicate,** under certain conditions (especially during a crisis of overproduction), may disintegrate into their component parts. A trust does not disintegrate so easily, since when it is formed, individual enterprises are deprived not only of commercial, but also of technical independence. The board of the trust, at its own discretion, closes some enterprises included in the trust and develops others. It moves the means of production from one factory to another, issues additional shares, and organizes new enterprises. An individual participant in a trust, just like any shareholder, has the right to demand payment of a dividend from the trust, but cannot demand the return of property transferred to the trust.

It is not difficult to see that all the **listed types of capitalist associations are nothing more than successive stages of capitalist concentration.** From ring to trust, from partial association to monopoly, from temporary to permanent—such is the path along which capitalist production proceeds from competition to monopoly, from anarchy to organization.

Each of these stages, each of the forms of capitalist associations, therefore, should not be regarded as something independent, as a kind of frozen system. Each of these organizations should be looked upon as a greater or lesser approximation to a monopoly.

Proceeding from the ring to the trust, capitalist accusations develop in depth and breadth.

On the one hand, the ties between the individual members of the associations are growing stronger and becoming more constant; on the other hand, each association strives to encompass all enterprises in a given branch of production. At the same time, this is accompanied by the integration and combination of capitalist industry. Capitalist society knows the two basic types of competition: horizontal competition, the struggle between homogeneous enterprises; vertical competition, the struggle between enterprises of different branches of production.

We encounter horizontal competition when we face a struggle between firms in the same branch of production over a buyer or a product. For example, the struggle of two textile enterprises with each other over a market, or their struggle over raw materials, labor, etc., are special cases of horizontal competition. The struggle of a textile enterprise with suppliers of raw materials, machinery, fuel, etc. is a case of vertical competition.

Vertical competition causes no less damage to the enterprise than horizontal competition. A textile enterprise cannot go bankrupt to the same extent both because a competitor (horizontal) has artificially lowered prices, and because suppliers of raw materials demand too high a price for this raw material. Vertical competition is one of the main reasons for the spread of capitalist associations from one branch of production to another. As soon as the capitalists employed in, say, the machine-building industry, by forming a cartel or trust, achieve a monopoly in this branch of production, an intensified desire for monopoly as a whole arises in a number of other branches. Having achieved a monopoly in the machine-building industry, the owners of machine-building plants raise the prices of machines enormously.

…. Ineligible

(statistical data)

In order to form a more or less correct idea of the system of monopoly organizations in pre-war Russia, one must not forget that, in addition to the frankly syndicate organizations, individual parts of the country's economy were interconnected by the so-called Representative Associations (C' ride entrepreneurs and their tips). Associations of this type were created, as it were, to protect the interests of a given branch of industry before legislative and governmental bodies. In fact, they often regulated the market and production by setting prices and coordinating the activities of individual cartels and trusts. For example, during the Imperialist War, the Council of the Congress of Mining Industrialists of Southern Russia set prices for coal, ore and iron, distributed labor power (prisoners of war) among entrepreneurs, received wagons for them, etc.

Thus concentrating in its hands all means of pressure on individual entrepreneurs, the Council of the Congress of Mining Producers of the South of Russia was a powerful association linking the entire industrial life of the south of Russia into a single whole. Here, a link was achieved between the activities of such powerful syndicate organizations as Prodamet, Produol, etc.

Associations of this type also existed in the mining industry of the Urals, in the flour industry, etc. There was also a united Council of Congresses of Industry and Trade.

Unfortunately, however, the activities of all these organizations have not been sufficiently studied. We shall not dwell in such detail on the consideration of capitalist associations in other countries. We will only point out that in Germany already in 1905 there were 385, and in 1918 over 500, all kinds of cartel organizations. In fact, these figures are somewhat underestimated since a significant part of the cartels existed illegally and semi-legally.

Among these cartel organizations there were a number of major cartels, of which the Rhenish-Westphalian Coal Syndicate, the German Steel Mills Association, the Electrical Companies Agreement, the Ceramic, Alcohol and Sugar Syndicates, and many others achieved a monopoly position in the market. Particularly significant was the development of the artel movement in the mining and chemical industries, however, a number of cartels also covered the manufacturing industries. At the same time, it should be noted that powerful trusts operated within these cartels and syndicates, which used the syndicate organization to fight small enterprises, but at the same time fought each other within the syndicate. Thus, giants were operating within the coal syndicate: the Gelsenkirchen Association, Germany, Luxembourg, Germany. Garten Island, Hyernia, Phoenix, Reinpresse, etc. Of the 63 million tons of total coal produced by the syndicate, 12 giants produced 48 million tons.

During the war, the syndicate movement in Germany intensified significantly, since the state, in order to regulate the market, forcibly syndicated a number of industries, and provided all kinds of support to the existing syndicate organizations.

After the war, when the German economy was in total ruin, the role of syndicates and cartels was significantly weakened. The general lack of goods in the country made syndicate regulation of the market unnecessary. During this period, the question of the supply of raw materials was much more acute, and from here all kinds of concerns grew.

After the stabilization of the German economy, the syndicate movement flared up with renewed vigor. The old syndicates are being restored and strengthened, and along with them new syndicate organizations are appearing. What is new in the German economy is the emergence of slaughter trusts. Among the associations of this type, we note only the most important ones. Here ptatsya: niline trust ("Joint-stock company of the industry of "drying substances" -" A. G. Farbeindustrie ".

*(statistical data)*

In the United States, the capital of the trusts at the beginning of 1908 amounted to the enormous sum of 35 billion dollars. The trusts extended their influence on the railway business and the main branches of industry. They monopolized the main branches of production: the production of iron and steel (Steel Trust), oil processing and oil trade (Oil Trust), smelting, copper, locomotive building, steamship building, telegraph, railways, electrical industry, tobacco production, production of agricultural machines, automobiles. , meat production and many others.

Even in England, the classic country of free trade, by the beginning of the century there were up to 100 largest cartels, each of which included at least 3/4 of the entrepreneurs in this industry.

In no country in the world has there yet been a case of any one trust taking over the entire production of the country with all its branches. So far, we have only known cases in which capitalist organizations achieved an absolute monopoly in individual branches of the country's production. However, the spread of monopoly organizations to individual branches of production does not prevent us from talking about the monopoly character of modern capitalist production as a whole.

Do not forget that linkage. between the activities of capitalist organizations is achieved by subordinating enterprises of the most diverse branches of industry, trade, and credit to the same financial centers. As an illustration, let us cite at least the following fact. On the eve of the war, the Franco-Belgian group of banks, which we have already mentioned above, controlled a very significant percentage of the capital invested in various branches of Russia's heavy industry.

*(statistical data)*

It goes without saying that all the listed branches of production, gravitating towards the same financial-capitalist center, obey its instructions and, thereby, are linked into a single whole.

Perhaps, the linking of the entire economic life of the country into a single whole will be shown more clearly by the famous scheme of John Moody, which characterizes the subordination of various branches of the economy of the United States (1906-1908) and their mutual interconnection (see p. 95).

A **capitalist association** (cartel, syndicate, trust, etc.) usually **includes** enterprises associated with various banks.

*(schematic)*

Individual banks are fighting among themselves for dominance in these organizations; however, at the same time, being interested in the success of their enterprises, they act in solidarity in all matters relating to the well-being of the industry associated with them.

The formation of cartels and trusts blurs the boundaries of individual concerns, the tentacles of individual banks are so intertwined. among themselves, which is difficult even for the banks themselves to determine which concern this or that enterprise belongs to.

"The Morgan and Rockefeller groups themselves are in close connection with each other. Morgan is the director of the main Rockefeller Bank ("New York City Bank"), the director and shareholder of a number of Rockefeller group enterprises.

Rockefeller, in turn, was until very recently one of the main shareholders and directors of the Steel Trust (Morganovskogo), several railroads and industrial enterprises adjacent to the Morgan group.

In many cases, it is even more difficult to distinguish whether this or that trust is adjacent to the Morgan or Rockefeller group, since among their leaders are representatives of both the first and the second.

### Financial capitalist state.

Up to now we have been talking about subordinating only the economic life of the capitalist countries to small groups of the biggest capitalists. It is not difficult, however, to show that not only the economic but also the political life of the peoples is in the hands of the same "capitalist oligarchy."

The immediate task of the capitalist state is, firstly, to protect the capitalist mode of production from encroachments on the part of the proletariat; secondly, the defense of the interests of the "national" bourgeoisie from the foreign bourgeoisie.

To carry out these tasks, the state maintains an enormous apparatus of class coercion and war: the army, the police, a network of state institutions, prisons, and so on.

The maintenance of all the people who are the constituent elements of the state apparatus, as well as the arming of the army and police, the organization of the fleet, etc. require huge annual expenditures from the state. To cover these costs, the state must also have corresponding revenues.

The state receives the funds it needs mainly through taxes, partly through the issuance of paper money and the organization of state enterprises.

Revenues flow into the state treasury more or less regularly. Expenses are not always regular. It often happens that at the moment when the state needs to make a large expenditure, there are not yet sufficient sums in the state's treasury.

There are also expenses that the state can cover only for a few years. For example, in order to keep up with its neighbors in this regard, the state needs to build a large number of huge ships at once or change all the weapons of the army. In such cases, the balance between state expenditures and revenues is disturbed, and the state is forced, sometimes, to resort to loans.

The state turns to the help of the private credit market. But the private credit market is, as we know, in the hands of a handful of monopolists. They are the ones who lend to the government.

However, by giving money, they put forward a number of conditions, they seek for themselves a number of privileges to change state policy in their own interests, to pass the laws they need, to replace a number of officials with candidates from financial circles, and so on.

The larger the loan, the more difficult the conditions that are imposed on the state.

The more often loans are made, the more often the state is subjected to pressure from monopoly circles.

Just as credit and industrial organizations of capital, credit and trade, credit and transport organizations are merging, the economic organizations of the bourgeoisie are merging with political organizations in exactly the same way.

Loans are one of the most powerful means, but not the only means of pressure of the banking sector on the state. We have already mentioned that the state draws part of the revenues; from the profits of their enterprises. It acquires its own mining enterprises, builds railways, organizes a post office, a telegraph office, and establishes large factories.

In order to finance all these enterprises, as well as to organize loans and to extract credit profits, the state organizes its own "state bank".

All these "state" enterprises, falling into an environment of private-capitalist monopolies, quickly fall under the influence of powerful private banking concerns and turn into their "offspring".

First of all, the state draws the capital necessary for the organization of these enterprises by issuing bonds. The private banks are buying up all these bonds and are turning the state enterprises into a means of generating income for the world. If these enterprises turn out to be unprofitable, the government pays the bondholders the income from its tax revenues. Private banks thus become, as it were, participants in the entire state economy.

The State Bank, along with private banks, carries out a variety of credit and financial transactions. Just like private banks, it takes part in the financing of industry.

As a result of these operations, his capital is so closely intertwined with private capital, so closely fused with them, that it positively merges with them into a single inseparable whole. "The example of the German "Reichsbank" (Reichsbank) is curious. This bank, whose economic role is enormous, is so closely connected with "private-economic" life that disputes are still ongoing: whether it is a simple joint-stock company or a state institution, whether it is of a private or public nature.

Finally, the state finds itself at the mercy of the financial, capitalist "top" in yet another respect: cannons, rifles, machine guns, warships, armored vehicles, uniforms for the army, police, and navy, in a word, all the attributes of a modern military predatory state, as well as thousands of items necessary for state industry and transport: rails, steam locomotives, steel, machinery, fuel, telegraph apparatus, etc., all this is produced by monopoly private-capitalist organizations.

The state's suppliers can dictate to it any prices for these goods, or, on the contrary, they can sell them "cheaply". For a concession, they demand, of course, a whole series of "favors".

Loans, financing of state industry, and state deliveries are the three powerful means by which the financial oligarchy tames the state, transforms it into a modest "political branch" of a powerful financial-capitalist trust.

Economically enslaving the state, the financial oligarchy consolidates its connection with it with the help of the tried-and-tested "system of personal union."

Suffice it to recall the tsarist Minister of Finance P. Bark, who played a major role in the Volga-Kama Bank, the former leader of modern Germany-Rathenau, who was at the same time the head of the famous "General Electricity Company", the recent Chancellor of Germany - Mr. Cuno, who was at the same time the director of the large steamship company Hamburg-America-Linien (Hapag), the German Minister of the National Economy Raumer, an employee of Stinnes, Jules Cambon, who was both a member of the board and vice-chairman of the largest bank Banque des Paris et des Pays Bas" and the chairman of the conference of ambassadors, or the Prime Minister of Great Britain-Baldwin, who at the same time is the owner of a large firm "Baldwin and. Co." and until recently was the director of the Bekas farm, ex. Minister of Finance, and now director of the largest English bank, Midland Bank, McCann, Secretary of the Treasury of the S. States, chairman of the aluminum trust. Mellon, and a thousand similar examples, in order to understand that the system of personal unions between the economic and political organizations of the financial bourgeoisie is a fact .

At present, **the career of a minister of the capitalist countries** is being made not in the offices of ministries and departments, **but in financial-capitalist enterprises.**

By **subjugating the state as a whole**, banking concerns, at the same time, seize its individual parts.**In addition**, they win over those of the major government officials who got to their post to them to their side, turn them into "their own people".

The history of recent decades knows many cases when major government officials, ministers, heads of departments, members of state councils, senators, and so on. received warm jobs in banking institutions or were otherwise **bribed by the financial oligarchy.**

The last elections in the United States, writes I.M. Goldstein, once again gave a whole series of evidence in favor of the fact that the old American proverb: to slip through American criminal laws in a carriage drawn by four," is quite reasonable. This was confirmed in his messages to Congress by the former President Roosevelt himself, comparing the billionaires: Rockefeller, Morgan, Harriman, Vanderbilt, and others with robbers on the highways and persons of other, even less honorable professions.

The last elections have shown that the trusts successfully bribed both the representatives of the liberal and the representatives of the democratic party. Despite the fact that Hearst published letters from the leaders of Standard Oil co, which established a number of under "ups" of major political figures, none of those bribed, as well as none of those who gave bribes, were brought to justice. James Bryce, who was England's Ambassador to the United States, wrote in his famous work on the United States that all legislative institutions that have to deal with trusts are more or less corrupt. In his opinion, about 5% of the members of both houses of Congress are directly accessible to bribery, about one-fifth is almost certainly open to corruption, and an even larger part can be suspected of dishonest acts.

Concerning the Massachusetts State Parliament in America

they say that the votes of the deputies of this parliament are traded in the markets in the same way as sausages or fish.

The political corruption created by the trusts is then seen from the following facts:

When, in 1905-1906, Hitchock, Secretary of State for the Interior, decided to annul the lease agreements concluded by Standard Oil with the help of government deceptions for the surrender of huge oil-bearing areas to Standard in Indian territory and in Okloram, Standard Oil Co mobilized a whole army of prominent representatives of various political parties.

Thus, for example, the cancellation of these leases was petitioned to Roosevelt by the Republican governor of New York, Niggins, the chairman of the national organization (i.e., the highest representative) of the Democratic Party-K. Jones, Pennsylvania Democratic President James M. Gutfey, and so on. Even more interesting is the case of Senator Bailey, who has long been known as a "tribune of the people" and an "enemy of the trusts", being in fact, as it turned out from his correspondence, in the service of Standard Oil Co.

Political corruption and terrorism of the trusts were no less sharply affected in the era of the last elections in the sense that many factories that did not work as a result of the crisis flaunted the inscription: "This factory will begin to work in 10 days after the election of Taft."

In other cases, the trusts threatened the workers, if Brian was elected, to close down the factories, lower wages, etc. How great the political influence of the trusts is further seen from the following facts: the present Secretary of State Knox was formerly the legal adviser of the steel trust, and Minister of Commerce and Labor Nagel was formerly legal adviser to Standard Oil Co in St. Louis.

Once quoted an excerpt from Goldstein's book made an impression. But can such facts surprise us now, when almost daily we learn much more instructive things.

Suffice it to recall the recent oil Panama in America, in which hundreds of deputies of both the Republican and Democratic parties, the largest ministers, the bribery of the "worker" Prime Minister of Great Britain-McDonald-by an automobile manufacturer, or, finally, the **dirty story of the Barmata** Concern **bribing the entire top of the German Social-Democratic Party and the Second International ...**

One of the powerful means of pressure from the financial oligarchy on the government and legislative bodies is the modern press.

"At present, the most powerful tool for mastering human souls is the press. He who is the owner of a large newspaper, or, as we have seen in the example of Stinnes, of a whole series of printed organs, concentrates in his hands a great social force. He can influence public opinion at his discretion, he is able to simulate public opinion where, in essence, it is not public but private interests that are at stake, he can, in the words of Lassalle, poison all sources of the national spirit and present the people spiritual death in its most varied form.

J. Caillaux, the former Prime Minister of France, and then the Minister of Finance, a battered, seasoned politician, characterizes the role of the press in the modern capitalist state in the following words: "In France, the government belonged or was owned to the strata of the petty bourgeoisie, sensible, moderate, peaceful-minded, undoubtedly not inclined to wide adventures, which can rather be reproached for being too predisposed to the trifles of everyday life, but concerned with maintaining the regime of freedom and law and order and striving to gradually improve the situation of the broadest strata of the population.

This reform work carried out by the petty bourgeoisie, however, met with resistance from the big bourgeoisie, which had united with the remnants of the tribal aristocracy.

After a long period when it had a predominant influence on the course of public affairs, the big bourgeoisie reached a position where its commitment to clericalism and its propensity for reactionary actions became clear to the whole country. Fleeing, thanks to the universal vote, her former hegemony, protesting in vain against this, finally realizing that there was no chance of making her majority in the chamber, she decided to resort to another tactic: to influence the decisions of the chamber, bringing them to the court of public opinion.

Strong in her education, which in a society that is not sufficiently democratized, is combined with the possession of money, she managed to take a strong position in some of the highest administrative institutions of the country. In this way, it exerted influence on parliament, could slow down reforms, and even influence the direction of foreign policy. But even under these conditions, **it could achieve only** insignificant results **if,** thanks to its financial power, **it did not seize a part of the press in its own hands** and did not meet **with support by the legitimate authorities.**

There is not a single informed politician who would not be aware of the change that has taken place in the last thirty years in modern journalism.

Small organs of one direction or another, which once grouped readers around themselves according to the parties to which they belonged, were supplanted by large informational organs.

And here the same thing happened that is happening in the industrial field and which we will repeatedly mention in the future. Massive citadels, rising up, destroy or suppress medium or small fortresses. A large enterprise demanding millions, the information organ inevitably becomes dependent on financially strong classes.

These latter, taking advantage not of civil liberty granted by law, but of the opportunity to show self-will, which was allowed by a democracy that did not want to implement the principles of firm power, created an instrument of new domination: they received the means to influence the legislative chambers, putting pressure on them through the press, which, following the instructions received, slandered, mocked the parties and their leaders, discredited, ridiculed parliamentarians and their proposals, governments and their projects.

The financial and tribal **aristocracies thus restored their influence on state affairs**; moreover, having seized power by a detour, **it did not assume responsibility for power.**"

"A **monopoly**, once it has taken shape and turns over billions, with absolute inevitability **permeates all aspects of social life, regardless of the political structu**re and of any other "particulars," wrote Lenin.

Having at their disposal **all means of pressure** on the authorities and public opinion, from powerful centers of financial capital-banks to newspapers and information agencies, from enterprises supplying weapons to schools and churches, the Morgans and Stinneses acquire in the modern capitalist state, regardless of the form of government, an unusually large specific gravity.

Even in an atmosphere of universal suffrage, direct, equal, and secret suffrage, **one Stinnes means much more than a million** workers and employees who receive their salaries and depend on it **in all manifestations of their existence**.

If the **capitalist state** has always been a tool in the hands of the bourgeoisie as a class, **now it is becoming not only** a "class tool of the bourgeoisie, but also **an organ of a small group** of capitalists who dominate the economic life of a given country.

It is interesting to note that in recent years, years of intense struggle and condensed politics, the financial-capitalist lords have more and more often found themselves forced to exercise their actual political power not through the mediation of the legitimate state apparatus, but directly appearing before the eyes of the masses as the sole masters of destinies. peace.

**Capitalist relations,** which have become more complicated as development progresses, **begin to simplify again.**

Let us recall the Genoa, Hague and Lausanne conferences, which were attended by the United States, instead of government delegates, by representatives of Morgan and Rockefeller; remember the London Conference, at which Morgan cynically and frankly dictated to the governments of the strongest powers a plan to appease Europe; let us recall the treaties with France and with the committee of experts which Stinnes concluded on behalf of Germany, informing his government of the results by a mere note; Finally, let us recall the history of the receipt by France of the last loan in America, and we will understand that political power, not only in substance, but partly even in form, passes to a handful of industrial and financial magnates.

**State apparatuses are increasingly becoming political branches** of the **economic organizations of the financial bourgeoisie.**

# IMPERIALISM

## Competition in the global market.

The economic life of **every highly developed capitalist country** is now covered by a single financial-capitalist organization. If every country were autarky [i.e. independently without the help of other countries, satisfies its needs] if it were isolated and not bound, the monopoly of capitalist organizations on national markets would be absolute. Competition and even exchange relations with all their attributes: prices, value, etc. would be completely ousted from modern society. The modern economy would cease to be capitalist and would turn into an organized blast society (Polobie of the slave-owning economy).

However, international relations are powerfully and rapidly developing from year to year. Increasingly large masses of goods rush from one country to another, giving rise to and developing into an international whole. Increasingly large masses of capital and labor force are migrating from one end of the world to another, strengthening and expanding international ties.

At present, there is not a single country in the world that could exist in isolation for a more or less long time. The experience of the last imperialist war, as well as the experience of the blockade of Soviet Russia, clearly confirmed this fact.

The modern economy, in its essence, is the economy of the world. Therefore, the extension of the power of financial-capitalist associations to entire countries does not eliminate competition from the system of modern capitalism. Quite the contrary.

As the power of individual capitalist organizations grows stronger, as their influence expands, competition in the world market becomes more and more fierce and destructive.

It must not be forgotten that each of the competing parties is now relying on the resources of entire countries and, moreover, acts hand in hand with powerful state organizations.

On the world market, as well as on national markets, the struggle between powerful capitalist trusts and concerns is waged along three main lines:

1) the struggle for markets,

2) struggle for raw material markets,

3) the struggle for capital investment markets.

**All these three types of competition** are closely connected with each other and represent, in fact, the **three sides of the single capitalist competition**. All these three types of competition, when transferred to the world market, lead to the **transformation of "peaceful" competition into armed competition**, lead to the **birth of imperialism** as an inevitable policy of modern states.

## Fight for markets.

There is an economic law that has long turned into a proverb, and is known to people, even completely unfamiliar with political economy: "demand causes supply." This short proverb contains, if you understand it well, a very large content. It indicates that with the modern development of technology, the production of any product can be brought to any size.

There would be demand, but you can always produce a product and in any quantity. Capitalist production knows no technical obstacles in its path. If it meets certain limits in each period, then these limits are set not by the technical impossibility of further expanding production, but by its economic unprofitability.

The goal of capitalist production is profit.

The capitalist constantly strives to increase the rate of profit. The first means of raising it is to improve the technique of the enterprise and increase the scale of production. At the improvement of the technology of the enterprise at full load, it gives a reduction in production costs, and at constant prices for the product, and an increase in the rate of profit. However, the prices of a product cannot remain unchanged in the domestic market if all entrepreneurs throw more products into the "national" market than before.

Therefore, the capitalists have to transport their surplus products abroad, to those countries where they can be sold for more favorable price. Thus, export abroad is generated not by an absolute overflow of the national market, but by a relative overflow. Surplus products can also be sold domestically; however, such a sale would lower prices, which the capitalists fear so much.

Where are the "surplus" goods from the highly developed capitalist countries going? The answer is self-evident—to countries less developed capitalistically, to countries where industry is not as highly developed and, as a result, prices are high.

However, "surplus goods are thrown away simultaneously from a number of capitalist countries. Every year the mass of commodities seeking external sales is rapidly growing, every year a "free market" is already becoming. Prices in the new markets are becoming more and more equal to the prices of the capitalist countries, and there are fewer and fewer places where goods can be exported at a higher price.

Each of the competitors, therefore, seeks to oust all its rivals from the world market in order to remain alone in the market. The price fight is on fire. Each of the rivals lowers prices in the expectation that the enemy will not stand it, go bankrupt and make room. The winner will be the one who can withstand low prices longer, who can sell goods on the world market for a longer time without profit.

Fierce competition for sales markets, a sharp struggle for the buyer and the price reduction resulting from this struggle in the old days always stimulated the improvement of technology.

In a modern monopoly society, on the other hand, where each of the competitors acts side by side with a powerful state apparatus and uses this apparatus as a weapon in the competitive struggle, the incentives for the improvement of technology are gradually dying out.

In this era, a completely new opportunity opens up for the entrepreneur to withstand the fierce struggle of prices without resorting to the improvement of production methods. This opportunity is created due to the spread of the system of offensive duties.

The system of customs duties existed in capitalist society even before the development of financial-capitalist relations. However, these were, as a rule, protective duties, the fundamental difference between which and modern ones is very great.

The purpose of the protective duty is to secure to the national industry such prices for goods as would provide the average entrepreneur with the recovery of production costs and the usual profit.

The purpose of the offensive tax is to raise domestic prices to the maximum and secure monopolistic super profits for monopoly associations.

Under conditions of free competition in the internal market, any duty, no matter how high it may be, turns into a protective duty since the struggle between domestic entrepreneurs and the transfer of capital into the most profitable industries always reduce the prices of each product to the level of the average production costs plus the average (national) rate of return.

We are saying here that monopolistic organizations inflate prices in the domestic market to the maximum limit.

It would seem that, under the condition of complete dominance in the market, capitalist organizations can raise prices indefinitely. In fact, this is not so.

 The profit of the capitalist depends not only on the height of the price, but also on the quantity of goods sold.

Meanwhile, any increase in the price of a commodity makes this commodity unavailable to more and more consumers and thereby reduces the demand for this commodity.

If the monopoly organization were to raise prices exorbitantly, it would increase its profit per unit of commodity, but at the same time it would be able to sell so little of the commodity that its gross profit would be reduced.

Assume that the cost of producing 1 pair of shoes is 8 rubles. The price of shoes fluctuates. In the same way, the demand for shoes fluctuates, depending on the price.

(...)

We see that the monopoly organization receives the maximum gross profit not at a maximum price of 25 rubles, but at a price of 17 rubles, which, while not being the maximum, still greatly exceeds production costs. It is at this level that the monopoly price is established.

It is necessary to note, however, one more feature. While in a pure capitalist economy the price of industrial products is determined by the average cost of production, the monopoly organizations inflate prices to such a level that it compensates for the cost of production and some profit even for the most basic of enterprises belonging to the association.

Here the price is thus determined by the cost of production, not under average conditions, but under worse conditions. As a result, more advanced enterprises receive additional differential profit (monopoly profit).

The state pursuing a policy of high customs duties acts here as an agent of monopoly associations. It is only **thanks to the assistance of the state** that the establishment of monopoly prices is conceivable. It is only thanks to the help of the state that the monopolist gangs are able to exploit the population of the country.

The monopoly profit received by the financial-capitalist groups **is not only their goal,** but, to a large extent, **also a means of competition in the foreign market.**

The monopoly profit received by the financial-capitalist groups is not only their goal, but, to a large extent, also a means of competition in the foreign market. Receiving huge premiums on the home market, the capitalist associations are able to export their goods abroad at significantly reduced prices. The internal premium makes it easier for them to compete with foreign rivals and often allows them to sell goods abroad at undoubtedly unprofitable prices.

"As an example, it suffices here to quote the history of the German sugar industry, which at the end of the 19th century exported about 3/5 of its production abroad. Since these exports were accompanied by large losses, the German sugar producers had to get high prices in the domestic markets.

When, therefore, in May 1900 they succeeded in creating a cartel covering 99.5% of the total sugar production in Germany, then immediately after this, prices in the home markets were immediately raised by 10%. The cartel, however, did not limit itself to this increase in its income; this is evident from the fact that while raw sugar was becoming cheaper and cheaper, the prices of refined sugar were kept at such a level that, with an artificial increase in them by 16-18 marks per 100 kilograms, German consumers had to annually overpay the sugar syndicate a huge amount of 100 million marks. An even more striking picture is in Russia's pre-war sugar industry. The famous Russian sugar syndicate achieved, with obvious support from the government, a complete monopoly in the domestic market.

Importation of sugar from abroad was completely stopped by high customs duties. This made it possible for the sugar syndicate to sell sugar domestically at 11-13 kopecks per pound (in retail trade), while production costs barely reached 5-6 kopecks. Inside the country, the syndicate thus earned up to 7 kopecks (more than 100 percent) on each pound of sugar. At the same time, on the world market, he faced fierce competition from Austro-German and especially English factories.

In order to bankrupt their main competitor, the syndicate sold Russian sugar to England at 8 kopecks per pound, which allowed English farmers to feed their pigs with Russian sugar, while the Russian peasant drank tea as a " «priglyadku» *(Russian proverb=without adding sugar, but only looking at sugar)*

The German nail industry sold half of its production abroad, with an annual loss of up to one million. It covered this huge loss with monopoly profits derived from the national market.

German beam factories sold their products in Italy for 30% cheaper than in Germany itself. The German Association of the Spirit Industry sold German alcohol abroad for 50% cheaper than at home.

The Russian oil companies followed the same tactics.

It is clear that the size of the internal "premium" received by monopolists depends not only on the height of monopoly prices, but also on the number of goods that can be sold at a monopoly price.

The larger the territory covered by the customs wall and given to the exploitation of a given group of monopolists, the more people live in this territory, the greater, all other things being equal, is the mass of monopoly profits received by them.

Therefore, representatives of large countries enjoy advantages in international competition, as they have the opportunity to shower foreign markets with masses of cheap goods.

If in the days of industrial capitalism the competitive possibilities of each entrepreneur, both in the domestic and foreign markets, were determined by the height of his technology, the perfection of the methods of production applied by him, now, in the days of monopoly finance capitalism, the size of the territory belonging to a given state organization plays a much larger role. 'unity, the size of the population covered by the customs wall.

Thus, the struggle for sales markets in an environment of monopoly capitalism gives rise to the desire of the monopoly organizations of the bourgeoisie (and, consequently, the states that have merged with them) to constantly expand the territory of their state, gives rise to the need for an aggressive policy for the capitalists.

Here, for the first time, we encountered the case when the state acts as an instrument of economic associations of the bourgeoisie in their competitive struggle.

And already this first case entails a change in the nature of competition, the extension of its sphere from the purely economic sphere to the sphere of international politics as well.

## Fight for raw materials markets.

The struggle for markets is thus the undoubted source of the emergence and development of imperialist policy. However, a much greater role in the birth of imperialism, as a system of international relations, is played by the struggle for raw material markets and, first of all, for mineral deposits.

Mineral deposits are limited by limits that, with the modern development of industry, cannot be considered inaccessible.

If we assume that the consumption of these essential items will no longer increase, then the world's coal reserves should last for 5,000 years, oil reserves for 40 years, iron reserves for 800 years. However, there is no reason to assume that, with a developing industry, the consumption of the main types of raw materials can turn out to be stationary.

Therefore, the terms of depletion of reserves should, in fact, be greatly reduced. However, if we were talking about the complete depletion of the world's mineral reserves, this issue could be considered topical only in relation to oil, the consumption of which is growing catastrophically, while the reserves are extremely limited.

Much more important is the question of the distribution of these reserves among the individual capitalist countries. It is known that lowering market prices is by no means the only method of competitive struggle. Along with it, a prominent place is occupied by the deprivation of the enemy of raw materials. Each of the capitalists strives not only to provide himself with raw materials, but also to keep his competitor out of the raw materials. Therefore, each of the monopoly groups participating in world competition strives to seize not only those raw materials that are necessary for its own needs, but also those that its opponent needs or may need.

That is why all deposits of oil, coal and all kinds of ores serve as objects of fierce struggle between the largest capitalist groups and the states merged with them. In these points of the globe, the appetites of all the major powers are cracked. These places turn out to be the nodes of the imperialist struggle.

It is known that one of the main reasons for the last imperialist war was the desire of the "ally" to deprive Germany of coal (the Saar and Ruhr basins, Upper Silesia) and iron (Alsace-Lorraine) and thereby undermine her economic might; and, on the other hand, Germany's desire to take possession of the French iron ore basin (Brieet department).

It is no less known that almost all major European conflicts that have arisen in recent years and threatened Europe with new military upheavals arose on the same coal-and-iron base (the Ruhr conflict, the Polish-German conflict, the Czech-Polish friction).

An important role in the World War was also played by the striving of the largest imperialist predators towards the oil basins: Germany towards Mesopotamia and Rumania, Great Britain towards Mesopotamia, and Persia.

The struggle for oil also played a significant role in the intervention of the "allies" in the Caucasus, and Japan in Kamchatka and Sakhalin in the development of the Greco-Turkish conflict, where England stood behind Greece, striving for Mossul, and Turkey was partially supported by France and the United States. States that did not want to let England into this rich oil basin.

The oil issue promises to remain the axis of international relations in the coming decades. The largest oil-consuming country, the United States (its consumption is about 70% of the world), is close to the complete exhaustion of its sources.

If The States will not want to become dependent on England, which has seized control of most of the world's oil reserves, they will have to make an attempt in the next few years to expand their oil possessions. And since England is unlikely to want to voluntarily release the enemy from the noose thrown around his neck, clashes over the oil issue seem inevitable.

Countries such as Mexico, Peru, Bolivia, Persia, and Mesopotamia will have to serve as subjects of fierce struggle in the coming years. However, along with minerals, raw materials supplied by agriculture are also the subject of fierce struggle. This branch of production in capitalist society, for reasons which we cannot dwell on here (reasons connected with the phenomena of rent), constantly lags behind the manufacturing industry in its development.

In capitalist society, therefore, there is a chronic shortage of agricultural products (bread, flax, cotton, and all kinds of foodstuffs). The prices for these products are constantly rising. However, this price increase cannot repulse consumers since they absolutely cannot do without these items. Because of the possibility of obtaining raw materials for industry in the required quantity, a fierce struggle flares up.

Each of the competing adversaries seeks to **secure for itself a sufficient number of sources of raw materials for monopoly** use, to which the adversary would not have access.

To this end, the monopoly associations are pushing the states associated with them onto the **path of capturing the agrarian countries.**

**Economic competition degenerates into competition for conquest.** Each of the competing countries is feverishly seizing "everything that lies badly", all the lands that do not have a specific owner.

*(statistical data)*

We see that every major power of modern times, striving to acquire a sufficient number of colonies, i.e. countries supplying raw materials for capitalist industry, is steadily increasing its "possessions". If two of the great powers: Russia and Germany have lost their colonial possessions, then the reason for this, of course, lies not in the absence of "evil will" among the imperialists of these countries, but in the revolution that turned the Russian Empire into a free union of peoples, on the one hand, and in the military defeat of Germany on the other.

## The export of capital.

However, perhaps the main root of imperialism is the third type of competition, characteristic exclusively of the era of financial capitalism - the struggle for the export of capital.

The division of the single world economy into a series of "national" economies by way of customs walls poses a whole series of almost insurmountable obstacles to international trade. The free movement of goods from one country to another is greatly hindered and, as a result, the equalization of prices in individual countries with the average world price is also difficult. Two completely identical enterprises in this situation bring their owners in different countries different profits. Deviations of the national rate of income (profit, loan interest, rent, etc.) from the average world rate are generated.

However, capital is always looking for the most profitable application. If it is not possible to export their goods to a country where prices are high, the capitalists export their capital there.

In other words, the capitalists of a country with a low rate of profit invest their free capital in the organization of enterprises not in their own country, but abroad.

Let us suppose that the German capitalist has free money capital at his disposal. If he invests his own capital in an enterprise in Germany, he will receive 15% of the profit. In Russia, prices are higher, and therefore the same enterprise will receive 20%. It is clear that the German capitalist would prefer to organize his enterprise in Russia rather than in Germany. He will take out his capital.

The **export of capital should not be confused** with the transfer (denationalization) of it. We encounter the export of capital **only when the owner of the capital does not move abroad** with his capital. Remaining himself at home, he sends only capital abroad and annually receives from abroad the surplus value created there.

**Three main forms of export of capital** must be distinguished: the export of capital that **yields entrepreneurial profit**, the export of capital that **yields interest,** and the **export of finance capital.**

If **a capitalist organizes an enterprise abroad** (industrial, commercial, credit, etc.), we are dealing with the **first type of export of capital.**

**If,** however, the capitalist, without organizing his own enterprise abroad, credits foreign industry, foreign governments, city administrations, etc., **we are dealing with the export of interest-bearing capital;** finally, we meet with the third type of capital export in those cases when the **capitalist exports his capital by buying foreign shares.**

All three types of capital export **play a very important role in the system of modern capitalism** and, in particular, **in the development of imperialism.** With the dominance of the joint-stock form of enterprise in the economic life of modern countries, the export of capital provides an opportunity for a large financial-capitalist association to subjugate the economic life of not only their own country, but also a number of other countries.

If, for example, a French bank buys shares in a metallurgical plant in the Donets Basin, it thereby exports its capital to Russia.

By buying a large number of foreign shares, as well as by founding "subsidiaries" enterprises abroad, a large bank can extend its dominance to a number of countries, include not only domestic, but also foreign enterprises in its sphere of influence.

In Russia, during the imperialist war, they shouted a lot about dominance, foreign capital. And, indeed, Russian practice provides a lot of material to illustrate the question of the dominance of the financial capital of one country in the economic life of others. In Russia there was, it seems, not a single branch of industry which, in one way or another, would not gravitate toward foreign centers of finance capital.

Let's start with the fact that all **Russian banks** (which, as we have seen, had achieved significant development, and had strong ties with Russian industry) **were in fact "subsidiaries" of large foreign banks.**

(*statistical data*)

However, Russian industry was directly connected with foreign capital.

Thus, Franco-Belgian capital almost completely dominated the Russian coal industry.

The subordination of Russian industry to him was so great that even the board of the powerful coal syndicate Produol, which freely regulated the Russian coal market, was located in Paris.

Things were little better in the Russian oil industry. By the beginning of the war, oil production in Russia was in fact concentrated in the hands of, or was under the control of, four of their largest companies: the Russian-American General Oil Company, the English Shell Company, the Dutch Royal General Company, and the Nobel Partnership.

The iron industry of Russia was almost wholly taken over by French-Belgian and partly by German capital.

The electrical and electrical engineering industries of Russia were wholly in the hands of two German companies: the General Electricity Company and Siemens & Schuckert.

Pre-war Russia is no exception.

The industry of all backward countries is in the hands of foreign capital, and even in the most powerful capitalist states foreign capital builds strong nests for itself. This can be seen at least from the following data characterizing the spread of American capital in Europe after the war.

"In Europe, Morgan's stronghold is, on the one hand, the English Schroeder Bank, and on the other, the largest French financial and industrial group, which includes: Schneider-Kreza and the Credit Lyonnaise and Union Parisien banks.

This is the same group with which Rockefeller's greatest rival, the Anglo-Dutch Oil Trust Royal Dutch, is associated. The Schneider-Creusot group, Union Parisien, has been extremely active after the war, buying up dozens of the largest enterprises in Lorraine, Luxembourg, Central South-East Europe, and the Balkans. The French wield a lot of Morgan capital. But over the past year, Morgan's bank has been acting more and more directly, making acquisitions on its own account.

"Morgan's capital is connected with two of the largest and most respectable banks in Austria - with Kreditanstalt and Bodenkreditanstalt. Through these banks, Morgan controls a large part of the Austrian industry. Among the enterprises that fell into direct dependence on Morgan, one should mention the famous largest Styrian Arms Factory, cartridge factories in Gartenberg, steel mills in Excessfeld, Krupp factories in Oernsdorf. According to some, not yet verified, data, Moran capital also penetrated the Austrian paper industry. Morgan also invaded the Galician oil industry, contacting one of the largest oil concerns - the Fanta concern. There is also information, although not completely verified, about Morgan's connection with Stinnes.

"Rockefeller is closely connected with German capital.

The sphere of influence of Rockefeller capital included German shipping, connected with the American concern Harriman, and the entire concern of the General Electricity Company, with groups adjoining it. But Rockefeller does not limit his activities to Germany. In France, he is also associated with a large bank - with the "Bank de Paris e Pay-Ba". Like Union Parisien, after the war, this bank developed an extremely vigorous activity in mastering the industry of central and southeastern Europe.

Investing in foreign enterprises is extremely beneficial for the financial-capitalist group that exports capital:

1) It gives it the opportunity to dispose of the social capital not only of its own country, but also of the capitals of other countries. To put it another way, the export of capital increases the amount of social capital at the disposal of a given financial-capitalist grouping.

2)  By exporting capital to countries with a higher rate of profit, the group exporting capital, of course, receives additional profit. However, of course, the most important thing for her is the fact that,

3)  3) penetrating into a foreign country and seizing its entire economic life in its own hands, it thereby makes its government dependent on itself. It entangles with the financial capitalist thread a whole series of states and is able to direct and regulate their policies in its own interests. it determines the policy of a given state; promotes its candidates for high government positions; seeks customs duties, etc.

Thus, **the export of capital** for the financial group replaces, albeit partially, the **expansion of the state territory of one's own country.** From this it is clear what fierce competition must flare up around the export of capital for investment in foreign enterprises.

The financial-capitalist grouping, which has subjugated the economic life of a large number of countries, disposes within these countries, as in its own internal market. Thanks to this, it receives great advantages in the struggle for markets, in the world price struggle. Each of the competitors, therefore, exports capital not only to those countries that give him high profits, but also to those countries where the attention of the enemy is directed.

It strives to paralyze every attempt of his rivals to master the economic life of this or that country and directs his steps wherever its opponent goes.

The **export of capital is thus not only an independent sphere of competition**, but also **an instrument of struggle** for markets for sales and raw materials.

No less powerful means is **the export of interest-bearing capital.**

Loan capital is exported, usually in the form of a loan to a foreign state or municipal administrations. It must not be thought that a finance-capitalist group, opening a loan to this or that government, receives only the interest on the loans, that the whole benefit derived from the loan is exhausted only by the receipt of the interest.

The loan is the surest means:

1) to extract large profits,

2) to penetrate into the economic life of the country,

3) to put pressure on a foreign government.

When opening a loan to the government of a foreign power, the banking concern stipulates a number of conditions.

It forces the credited government to abolish all kinds of customs slingshots against its goods and to sharpen the customs struggle against its competitors. It obtains from the credited government large orders for products of his production (mainly for weapons, rail iron, steam locomotives, etc.).

It demands that he be granted profitable concessions (for the construction of railways, telegraph lines, for the development of deposits of coal, ore, oil, for the exploitation of forests, etc.). It forces the government to be credited to conclude commercial, political, and military treaties with the crediting country.

In certain cases, It even receives the right to reorganize the army of the country being credited (in which case all leading command positions are filled at It discretion), the right to control the country's finances, over its railways, and so on.

There are a lot of examples of such agreements both in pre-war and post-war practice.

The Russian tsarist government, instead of the one received after the 1905 revolution. loan in France, made orders for warships to French factories. The Serbian government, after receiving a loan from France, stopped its military orders to Austrian factories (Skoda, Mannlicher, etc.) and purchased armaments exclusively in France (French firms in 1908-1911 delivered war materials worth 45 million francs to Serbia).

Under the pressure of these same loans, for several years it waged a fierce customs struggle against Austria.

*(statistical data)*

The export of capital by loan is thus a powerful means of enslaving foreign states.

It is at the same time a profitable field for the investment of capital, it is an instrument of competition in the market for the sale of raw materials and the investment of industrial capital, and serves as an instrument in international political and military competition.

### The rebirth of capitalist competition.

#### Militarism

On the world market, large banking concerns act as competitors, each of which dominates the economic life of a number of countries and has the armed power of a number of states.

Competition extends decisively to all areas of life where the interests of competitors may collide.

First of all, there is industrial competition, with each of the competitors striving to strengthen and develop its industry indefinitely and weaken the industry of its rivals.

At the same time, there is a struggle for raw materials markets and capital investment markets. This struggle is connected with the desire to expand one's territory and entails "competition of conquests."

The struggle for territory requires each side to strengthen its armaments, and this sphere becomes an independent sphere of competition. Each of the competitors strives to be stronger than the others. The arming of one entails the strengthening of the other.

In order to expand its possessions, each power needs to have an armed force - an army and a navy. Since the big capitalist powers in their policy of conquest encounter only the resistance of the populations of the backward agrarian countries whose territory they encroach on, they do not have to excel in armaments for this purpose: a small handful of people armed with firearms is enough to break the resistance of the largest countries that have not embarked on the path of capitalist development.

It suffices to recall how handfuls of armed Spaniards and Portuguese conquered America in the 15th-16th centuries, or how in the 19th century almost all (90%) of Africa was divided among the major European powers for 25 years, to make sure of this completely.

However, as the possessions of the capitalist states expand, there are fewer and fewer "free lands" left on the globe. The appetites of a number of the biggest capitalist competitors rush to the same plots of land. And now, in order to acquire one of these "scraps", the capitalist power has not only to overcome the resistance of the local population, but also scare off with an armed hand all competitors who claim to seize this tidbit.

As an example, let us cite the following case: in 1878, Russia succeeded in the "Liberation" war to crush the resistance of Turkey. The traditional aggressive-imperialist policy of tsarist Russia, aimed at conquering Turkey, is close to being realized. March 3, 1878 Russia concludes peace with defeated Turkey in San Stefano, according to which Turkey was almost completely expelled from Europe.

But here Germany, on the one hand, and on the other, England, Russia's longtime rival in relation to the Turkish heritage, entered the scene. England mobilized the fleet; the lower house voted war credits; all-out military preparations began.

England declared that she demanded a revision of the San Stephans treaty, otherwise she would go to war with Russia. In Russia, passions flared up. At first, Russia was, as it were, ready to accept a war with England.

But Bismarck (Chancellor of Germany) "friendly" warned against this risky step. Russia was forced to submit, and the famous "Berlin Conference" was convened in Berlin.

Russia's conquests were cut to a minimum; on the other hand, England, Germany, Austria, and other powers, who did not take any part in the war, profited greatly.

In order to make conquests in such a situation, it is necessary to have an armed force not only sufficient to carry out the seizure, but also capable of silencing any competitor. A sharp competition in arms begins. Each power strives to be stronger than any of its opponents, and, if possible, all opponents taken together.

Arms competition associated with the competition of conquests escalates especially strongly by the beginning of the 20th century when the entire globe turned out to be divided without remainder. By this time, there were no "free" lands left, each piece of land has its own "owner".

The entire territory of the globe suitable for human habitation is 134 million square kilometers. From this territory in 1914 r. belonged to:

*(statistical data)*

In order to expand its possessions, each power now has to wrest the acquired plots of land from the hands of a more or less powerful enemy, at the same time encountering the resistance of all competitors.

That is why, since the end of the last century, and especially since the beginning of this century, the **growth of armaments has taken on catastrophic proportions.** All states strain their budgets to the point of impossibility in order to keep up with their rivals in armament.

The following table shows the rise in military spending by the largest imperialist states of Europe on the eve of the war.

*(statistical data)*

For 30 years, the costs of European states for the war have more than doubled. However, tsarist Russia (which increased its military budget by more than 3 times), Great Britain (almost keeping up with Russia in this respect) and Germany (more than doubling its military spending) show especially intensive growth in military spending. The absolute figure for the military expenditures of the six powers over the entire period is enormous, it amounts to 8% of the value of all the property of these countries in 1914.

Comparison of military spending with the total national income suggests that at least 4-5% of the total national income of the capitalist countries was annually spent on military purposes.

In 1909-10, as can be seen from the following table, about 10 rubles of military expenditure fell per capita in the main capitalist countries.

*(statistical data)*

The **imperialist war,** whose ostentatious **slogans were the struggle for peace, the defense of freedom** and culture, not only did not put an end to this waste of the people's wealth, but, **on the contrary**, contributed to an even **greater increase in armaments.** This can be seen at least from the following figures.

*(statistical data)*

The total number of armies of the most important 16 states reached on the eve of the war (in peacetime) a huge figure of 6,000,000 people.

*(statistical data)*

Despite the almost complete disarmament of the defeated countries, the size of the armies has not been reduced, since the victorious and neutral countries keep under arms much larger masses of troops than before the war. By the end of 1923, there were 6,315,280 people in the ground armies all over the world (excluding the USSR). Thus, the years of the post-war peace did not lighten the burden of militarism.

We will not dwell in the same detail on the naval armaments of the capitalist powers. In parallel with the growth of land armaments, both the number of warships and their size are growing.

**Each of the capitalist powers strives to overtake the other in its armaments**.

At the same time, it is ridiculous to look for the perpetrators of the militaristic fever in the face of this or that state.

The very nature of competition in the epoch of monopoly capitalism obliges each imperialist power to multiply and increase its military might indefinitely. Each state, being surrounded by armed neighbors, ready to attack it at any moment and take away from it all the seized property, is forced to arm itself.

However, his armament; in turn, alarm the neighbors and force them to produce new weapons. **Armed competition is degenerating into arms competition.**

If in the epoch of imperialism armaments are in themselves only an instrument of struggle for sales markets, raw materials, and investment of capital, then **armed competition,** turning into an independent field of competition, can **also become a cause of war.** The sibilance of this or that power is a constant threat to its competitors, and it is not surprising that they seek to take advantage of every moment **when the balance of forces develops in their favor** in order to **put an end to their rival by war.**

There is reason to believe that such reasons played no small role in the emergence of the war of 1914-18.

However, **arms competition is not limited** to competition **in the number of armies** and navies or in the quality of their weapons. **Each power seeks to occupy the most advantageous strategic position** possible.

Therefore, the attention of all opponents is directed to all points on the globe, which, by virtue of their geographical position, can be of strategic importance. And in their striving towards the same points on the globe, the **capitalist powers inevitably collide with** each other.

It is known, for example, what role in the last imperialist war and in most conflicts of the late 19th and early 20th centuries was played by the struggle for mastery of the "straits") - the Dardanelles and the Bosphorus. Russia, and Germany, and England, and Austria simultaneously aspired to this narrow strip of land. Meanwhile, these straits had **more political than economic significance** for each of the contending parties. Russia needed the straits to get rid of the threat of penetration of foreign fleets into the Black Sea. Germany, for the construction of the strategic Baghdad road and for military pressure on Russia and Turkey.

England, for dominance in the Black Sea and for countering the aggressive plans of Germany and Russia, etc. We see that militarism, generated by competition for markets, raw materials, and capital investment in conditions where the instruments of competition are **not only economic, but and political means,** itself turns into an independent field of competition and becomes a source that **strengthens the imperialist, predatory tendencies** of modern states.

**Imperialism as a policy of financial capital.**

The pacifist "Marxists", led by Kautsky, while paying tribute to the humane indignation against the military policy of recent decades, nevertheless believe that imperialism is not an inevitable companion of finance capitalism. They are engaged in composing wise projects, during which "peaceful" competition in the world market would become possible. However, they forget that life is not subject to good wishes, that elemental laws do not depend on the will of good old people.

Whether the "Marxists", who emasculate all of its revolutionary content from Marx's theory, wish it so, or not, **the actual subjects of the world economy,** the actual participants in world competition, are the capitalist organizations, uniting in their hands **both the economic and political life of the peoples**, relying both on the economic and military power of entire countries. **It is not surprising that in the fierce struggle** for mastery of the markets, they use all the means available to them.

**No competitor gives up** until he has used all the means of resistance at his disposal. That is why the decisive method of competition in the world market is war.

The process of concentration of capital on a global scale **is unthinkable** without long and inevitably repeated wars. **War** here is **an instrument for the concentration of capital**, and by no other means can the process of concentration of capital on an international scale be carried out in conditions where the economic organizations of the bourgeoisie are fused with its political organizations.

**Also unthinkable** is the consistent centralization of capital on a world scale, through the creation of stable world capitalist associations. World monopoly associations were already in existence before the war. Thus, the trade in aluminum, which plays a very important role in military affairs (especially in aviation), was in the hands of a single trust. An international syndicate (consisting of German and S.-American enterprises) also monopolized the entire world zinc market was divided into spheres of influence (between the Rothschild, serving Europe, and the American syndicate) the world nickel market.

The platinum syndicate concentrated in its hands not only world trade, but also the entire world production of platinum. On the eve of the war (in September 1913), an international cartel of steel and iron was formed - the Iron and Steel Institute, which covered all the countries producing steel and iron, but did not have time to show itself, as it existed only 10 months.

The International Rail Syndicate united in its hands 1/5 of the entire world production of rails. Maritime shipping was also dominated by an international syndicate. Before the war, the electrical industry of the whole world was dominated by two huge trusts: the German "General Electricity Company" and the American "General Electric Company".

These two trusts entered into an agreement between themselves in 1907, according to which markets were divided between them and competition was eliminated.

A number of international associations still exist today.

*(statistical data)*

We see, therefore, that some of the international associations are creating an elaborate organization. However, **despite this**, we argue that the **centralization of capital on a world scale** is extremely **difficult and limited.**

The **main obstacle** on this path lies **in the law of uneven development of capitalism.**

Capitalism always develops unevenly. However, **in the era of imperialism,** when all the contradictions of capitalism are revealed with particular clarity and sharpened to an extreme degree, **this law operates with particular force.**

In the era of imperialism, we observe a slowdown in the rate of development of the oldest industrialized countries.

This slowdown stems from three main sources:

1) The presence of old industrial equipment in these countries makes it difficult for them to improve the production apparatus. With the advent of new, improved machines and devices, the capitalists of these countries cannot immediately scrap all the old equipment of enterprises. Only as old machines wear out can they gradually replace them with new ones. Moreover, the higher the organic composition of capital (and, as we know, it rises in the course of capitalist development), the slower is the replacement of old equipment with new.

2) The spread of monopolies in the most advanced capitalist countries, as we have seen, weakens the incentives for the improvement of technology and gives rise to a tendency towards the technical decay of capitalism.

3) The very essence of finance capitalism leads to the fact that the vast masses of surplus value, extracted by the capitalists of the most powerful capital countries from the exploitation of the proletariat and numerous colonies, are invested in the industry of these countries to a lesser extent and are exported abroad in greater quantities in the form of capital.

This causes a tendency **to turn the most economically powerful powers into rentier states**.

On the other hand, **backward countries** that are just embarking on the path of **capitalist development show a much faster pace** of industrial growth. The import of capital from abroad gives rise to ever greater **investments of capital in industrial enterprises**, railways, etc.

The **absence of old equipment** makes it possible to build enterprises according to the latest technology.

The combination of high technology with cheap labor stimulates the rapid growth of capitalism.

In the course of capitalist development, there is a constant change in the share of individual capitalist states in the world economy. First one, then another country **suddenly begins to develop an increased pace** of development and is put forward among the leading countries of the world.

Thus, in the decades leading up to the war, Germany not only went through a rapid transformation from an agrarian to an industrial country, but in many respects surpassed England, that classical country of capitalism. The United States of America, until recently a backward agrarian country, has outstripped both England and Germany in its capitalist development. Agrarian Japan has also come to the fore among the first-class imperialist powers.

In the post-war period, Canada, Australia, South America, India, and to some extent China, showed a frantic pace of capitalist development, which in their development threaten to overtake and overtake the European countries.

These constant shifts in the correlation of forces of the capitalist states lead to a sharp intensification of imperialist emulation and are one of the main causes of imperialist wars.

They also make **any stable international associations of capitalists inconceivable.**

When a world association is formed, the markets are distributed among the participants in proportion to the capital of each of the parties included in the association. Meanwhile, individual countries are developing at different rates. While the economic power of some countries is developing very slowly, other countries are developing, indeed, by leaps and bounds. Hence the need for a **constant revision of the shares of each** individual country in world production, which causes inevitable discord between the participants in international associations and their inevitable collapse.

*(statistical data)*

The **formation of international associations** does **not eliminate arms competition.**

On the contrary. It in itself is a stimulus to the **strengthening of armaments**. The fact is that, when an international syndicate is formed, the distribution of markets and shares of participation in world trade is based not only on the economic, but also **on the military power** of individual participants.

Therefore, upon conclusion of an agreement, each participant, in order not to lose his share and, if possible, to increase it, is forced **to increase his military** might.

The moment he is strong enough to renegotiate the agreement in his favor, he presents the syndicate with ultimatum demands and, if they are not satisfied, blows up the syndicate.

**Thus**, international syndicates, firstly, are not very strong and, secondly, **are powerless** to stop competition in the world market.

International trusts are somewhat stronger; however, they find a very weak distribution for themselves, because they encounter almost insurmountable obstacles in the way of their formation. The formation of a trust is possible only **if** the profits of individual participants do not decrease, **but increase** during its formation.

Meanwhile, in modern capitalist society, divided into parts by customs walls, the rate of profit in individual countries is far from being on the same level. In backward countries, as a rule, the rate of profit is much higher, while in developed countries it is lower. When enterprises merge into a single trust, profits are usually distributed among individual participants in proportion to the capital invested by them. However, here such a distribution would be extremely disadvantageous for the capitalists of the backward countries and extremely advantageous for the capitalists of the advanced countries.

That is why not all capitalists agree to the formation of international trusts, and these organizations do not find wide circulation. Not a small obstacle is also the uneven development of technology in different countries and the resulting inequality in the organic composition of capital.

The **elimination of military policy** from the system of modern capitalism, therefore, turns out to be **completely unthinkable**.

War remains the decisive method of **concentrating capital** on a world scale; **imperialism remains the inevitable policy of finance capital.**

## Imperialism as the last stage of capitalism

Hence arises an essential contradiction which threatens the capitalist system with inevitable destruction.

The productive forces of the world have reached such a high level that production can only exist in the form of world production. A strict division of labor develops between the individual countries of the world, which makes absolutely necessary the free exchange of substances between them. Free international trade, free flow of capital and labor from one country to another becomes a condition without which no country in the world can exist.

The inviolability and continuity of international relations is becoming a necessary condition for the possibility of reproducing the world's productive forces.

A single world economy requires a single economic organization.

Meanwhile, the organization of the economy under the system of finance capitalism and imperialism remains inevitably fragmented. The world economy is divided into a number of state associations, each of which, guided by the interests of competition, pursues a protectionist policy, fences itself in with a customs wall, and in every possible way hinders the free exchange of substances between individual states.

The world economy requires a unified organization. However, we have seen that capitalism is unable to create such a unified system by peaceful means. In the ruins of capitalist society, there is only one means by which it tries to create a single world economic organization. This tool is war.

From a certain point of view, every imperialist war is an instrument of capitalist concentration. **The goal of any war is to eliminate one competitor** or a number of competitors from the world market. The war should reduce the number of states **taking part in the world competition** and expand the limits of each of the lagging states.

As a result of wars, the number of states dividing the world economy among themselves must decrease **until, finally, one state covers** the whole world. **Imperialist wars are thus an attempt to create a single capitalist organization** of the world economy, an attempt to eliminate the basic contradiction between the level of the productive forces of the world economy and **its capitalist superstructure.**

It is not difficult, however, to see that all these attempts are doomed to failure in advance.

An attack on one major power or another inevitably draws all the major powers of the world into the war. Under such conditions, the **destruction of one of the competitors by military means becomes completely impossible**. A war between two major competitors **will inevitably turn into a war between coalitions** of the largest states in the world.

If we take into account that each of these powers has colossal economic and military power, it becomes quite clear that such a war cannot be short-lived, it inevitably turns into a long, stubborn, and fierce struggle.

This protracted nature of modern imperialist war makes it completely unsuitable as an instrument of capitalist concentration. The war is tearing the world economy apart for a long period of time, interrupting international relations for a number of years. Meanwhile, we have seen that the continuity of international relations is an indispensable condition for the existence and development of modern states.

By the mere fact that the war is connected with the rupture of international relations, it leads the world economy to ruin. Industrialized countries are deprived of sufficient quantities of raw materials and foodstuffs and consequently reduce their production. The agrarian countries are experiencing a shortage of agricultural machinery and other industrial products.

This exhaustion is increased all the more because **war requires a colossal unproductive waste of valuables**. The industry of all countries of the world during the war expands the **production of items of military equipment at the expense** of civilian consumption items.

An increasing part of the labor of the whole world is spent on the production of cannons, machine guns, military airplanes and ships, poisonous gases, barbed wire, and other items that perish irrevocably on the battlefield.

Enormous armies consume tens of millions of poods of grain and meat, wear out an incalculable amount of footwear uniforms, etc., while they themselves produce absolutely nothing.

The losses of the world economy caused by a protracted war are seen in the example of the last imperialist war.

*(statistical data)*

To this number must be added, of course, the huge armies that had to be kept under arms, just in case, by the neutral countries.

Further, here we must add tens of millions of workers who during the war in all countries were employed in enterprises working "for defense."

A good 90,100 million people were thus cut off from peaceful production. Of the 63 million mobilized, mankind has lost: 10.2 million killed and 21 million wounded.

However, this does not exhaust the loss of humanity. The ebb of a huge number of men to the war led to a colossal reduction in the birth rate. The malnutrition and disease that accompanied the war caused a severe increase in mortality. The reduction in the birth rate is determined by 21 million people, the increase in mortality by 6,000,000.

In total, mankind lost 37 in the war. The war cost the Entente powers 510 billion gold marks (or about 350 billion gold rubles).

The war caused a reduction in all major industries, as evidenced by the following table:

(statistical data)

If we do not take into account the accidental large wheat harvest in 1918, but judging by all the war years, it will turn out that only steel production gives an increase during the war. This increase is equal to 2.5 million tons.

If, however, we take into account that tens of millions of tons of steel, cast iron, and coal were used for military needs, it becomes clear that the peaceful consumption of these items has been greatly reduced.

The production of Europe was especially hard hit, as can be seen from next plate.

(statistical data)

The matter cannot, however, end in war alone.

As we have already pointed out, in the imperialist struggle, entire groups of states are fighting on both sides of the trenches. Even if, as a result of a war, the capitalist world succeeded in completely destroying one of the contending groups, then even in this case the **capitalist economy would not be concentrated in the hands of a single subject** and armed competition would not cease.

In the course of the war, **the uneven development of capitalism is exacerbated.**

Some countries suffer more from war, others less. At the same time, countries that do not take part in the war or participate in it only indirectly grow richer and begin to develop intensively.

New competitors emerge from among these countries. Individual members of the coalition must inevitably clash with each other or with newly born competitors.

The first war must be followed by a second, the second by a third, and so on. The power of the adversaries who clash with each other in armed conflicts must increase from time to time, and at the same time, wars must become more and more destructive.

**Entering the era of finance capital**, humanity thus **entered the era of periodically recurring wars.**

And the era of wars inevitably leads to a halt in the process of development of the productive forces, for any progress of the productive forces, any accumulation of the power of mankind in relation to nature is brought to naught by the subsequent war.

From a progressive system facilitating the constant development of the productive forces, capitalism in the era of imperialism is transformed into a system that hinders the development of the productive forces and retards the difference of mankind.

Monopoly capitalism is a class system, a system built on the intensified exploitation of the proletariat and the multimillion colonial peasantry. Arousing the hatred of the vast majority of the population of the world, it is able to hold out only so long as all the forces of powerful state apparatuses are concentrated on suppressing any discontent on the part of the oppressed masses.

The era of war brings this system out of balance. It increases the dissatisfaction of the working masses, demanding from them, in addition to the usual hardships, colossal human sacrifices and eliminating even the appearance of "concerns" of the metropolises about the colonies. At the same time, wars divert the forces of the capitalist states to interstate struggle and in every possible way undermine the apparatuses of oppression of all the capitalist groupings participating in the war.

Capitalism succumbs to the blows of the proletarian revolution and national uprisings much earlier than it has time to arrive at a single organization of the world economy.

It is not capitalism that is destined to create this organization, but the social system that is coming to replace it and whose ghost has long hovered not only over Europe, but over the whole world.